D0563995

NEW GUIDE

TO THE

PRADO GALLERY

OVIDIO-CESAR PAREDES HERRERA
Doctor en Filosofía y Letras

NEW GUIDE
TO THE
PRADO GALLERY

Foreword by the
EXCMO. SR. MARQUES DE LOZOYA

Translated by
JOHN MACNAB CALDER

EDITORIAL MAYFE, S. A.
Ferraz, 28
MADRID (8)

© EDITORIAL MAYFE, S. A.

MADRID

15.ª edición

Printed in Spain
1973

Depósito legal: BI. 838-1973
I.S.B.N.: 84-7105-088-9

Artes Gráficas Grijelmo, S. A. Uribitarte, 4 - Bilbao

FOREWORD

I must confess that the idea of «Art Gallery» conveys a rather ambiguous feeling to mind. In itself, it is not a notion that I care for much, implying as it does the massing together of art treasures which have been carried off from the places for which they were intended, and have been set out and classified with instructional aims that rob them of much of their appeal. And yet, the Art Gallery is just the place where the work of art is isolated from all the «anecdotic» values that tended to smother it in its original site, and where it delivers itself up to our enjoyment stripped of all false prestige, and with no value other than its own intrinsic beauty. It is true that when we go to see «The Burial of Count Orgaz» where it hangs in a chapel of a Toledo church, our sensitivity for the discovery grows sharper as we pass through the narrow Moorish streets on the way; but it is no less true that the same picture in an aseptic room in an Art Gallery would triumph by its beauty alone, with no need of aid from the memory of mudéjar minarets or Renaissance grilles.

The Prado Gallery is perhaps the only one in which both modes of enjoyment are possible with the truly astonishing quality and quantity of works of art that are here assembled. They are presented to our contemplation in didactic order, but in an atmosphere uniquely steeped in poetry. It is the building itself, of *a classicism already sensitized by the first Romantic arms, with the harmony of its bluish granite columns: it is the atmosphere of the halls and rooms, with their vaulted ceilings and rotundas, amid which we feel as tiny as those human figures inserted in the old engravings to show the proportions of architecture by contrast. The Prado is free from any educational obsession, and in it we feel as we should in the saloons of a palace or the naves of a cathedral. It is not something created by a law devised for the increasing of a citizen's culture, like those drafted in bureaucratic prose by the Ministers of Louis Philippe or Napoleon III. It is the private collection of the great* amateurs *who were Kings and Queens of Spain, made over to the people by one of them who perhaps was incapable of loving or understanding anything but beautiful pictures. That is why the atmosphere of the Prado is unusual. I suppose that only the Ermitage Gallery in St. Petersburg —not Leningrad— could yield a similar sensation. He who has time to see the Prado as the great Museums and Galleries should be seen, needs no guide. He should go back again and again, never for too long at a time, to go through it all, little by little, and to comprehend all it contains; there are about twenty pictures in the Prado that deserve the honour of a special visit devoted to each one of them alone. Privileged visitors of this kind need nothing to read but the nameplates at the bottom of the pictures. But there are others —the majority— who must go over the whole of the Prado in a few hours. And they do need a guide, whether of flesh and blood or of paper, to steer them through the intricate labyrinth of rooms and halls, and, more important still, to show them what must not be missed, by pointing out the most interesting items for a quick survey and a better understanding.*

Ovidio-César Paredes Herrera, who has devoted his youth to the study of art, offers to be our kindly guide. His keen sense of observation, and his magnificent training, which marks him out as a true connoisseur in art matters, are to be found in this simple book, filled with niceties of observation. This is not a learned treatise or a catalogue; it is simply a counsellor, a faithful friend, which will suggest itineraries by drawing your attention, with a judgement that is always reliable, to those works before which you ought to halt for a little while. It is also a pleasant reminder of your visit, which perhaps in your distant home will always be ready to converse with you, and to recall the feelings of a few hours in what is possibly the choicest atmosphere that can be breathed on earth.

MARQUES OF LOZOYA.

THE PRADO GALLERY

The Museo Nacional de Pintura, formerly known as the Museo Real and commonly called the Prado Gallery, placed in one of Madrid's finest avenues, the Paseo del Prado, from which it takes its name. The building, unadorned but tasteful, and regarded as one of the best of its kind in Europe, is a short distance from the Plaza de la Cibeles; it has the Botanical Garden on one side, and of San Jerónimo el Real's church behind, with trees and gardens of the Buen Retiro Park further up the hill.

The out side in harmonious neo-classical style, without some elaborate Baroque decorations, and the building is an eleganted one of three storeys and four façades, forming a parallelogram 585 feet long by 117 deep. The main frontage consists of a double gallery, with a handsome Doric portico in the middle. Columns, semicircular arches and figures adorn the whole façade of the lower gallery, in which Doric and Ionic features are gracefully and harmoniously combined. In front stands a large statue of Velázquez, with broad lawns on either side.

The south façade, facing the open space with the

statue of the painter Murillo, is the less architectural importance, with the Corinthian order predominating; the one best known to visitors, however, is the northern, beside the Ritz Hotel, with the monument to Goya in front of it.

This façade has two entrances, one giving access to the lower floor and another door higher up, approached by a double staircase in granite, of modern construction, which ends at the entrance-door, framed in a peristyle resting on two Ionic columns.

The execution of plans for the building was entrusted to the distinguished Madrid architect Juan de Villanueva in the reign of Charles III, to whom, in 1787, he presented his plans for a Natural History Museum.

Charles IV proceeded with the work, and afterwards the damage done to the building during the Peninsular War was repaired.

Ferdinand VII finally decided to make it a national picture gallery, and continued the task of restoration and adaptation; he personally inspected the works and supervised the arrangement of the rooms.

After several postponements, the Gallery was officially opened on 19 November 1819; it then contained rather more than 300 pictures, and a considerable stir among connoisseurs was caused.

Extension works on the building were continued by Ferdinand VII, and royal decrees and orders brought fresh contributions to its rooms.

During subsequent reigns, the collections became more complete, through donations, bequests from private persons, and purchases with the Gallery's own funds.

In May 1956 the Gallery premises were extended by the opening of fifteen new rooms, four of which were double, in two wings built in the former garden by the architects Sres. Chueca and Lorente.

In this new arrangement the position of many works has been altered, and it has been sought to assemble pictures by great painters which were formerly dispersed in different rooms and on different floors. This makes it possible to follow the work of the chief masters in a more orderly manner, and obtain a more complete idea of their work.

Thus, the work of **El Greco** can now be seen in three consecutive rooms; that of **Velázquez, in six;** that of **Goya,** in nine, in addition to the rotunda at the end of the Central Gallery; that of **Veronese,** in two, and those of **Van Dyck, Brueghel «de Velours», Murillo, Ribera,** and others, in spacious halls.

New premises in the semi-basement have recently been thrown open to the public, comprising two rooms devoted to British and Dutch paintings, and the lecture room which will also be fitted up for temporary exhibitions.

The pictures are generally hung by schools and authors in a sound distribution of Rooms, which fit in with the layout of the building and are clearly and conspicuously marked with Roman numerals. The new Rooms bear the same number as the Rooms to which they are attached, with the addition of the letter A, except for Room XV.

The Management pays the greatest attention to the preservation and repair of the pictures, the condition of which is perfect on the whole, despite the action of time and the quality of the colours, which in some cases are rather impermanent.

Constant needs for restoration, and the climatic conditions of Madrid, frequently call for the withdrawing of pictures from the rooms, and the closing of one or more rooms during the hot months.

Nearly all the paintings in the Prado are done in

oils, but there is one piece of Romanesque fresco and a few works in tempera, and the lower rooms contain a few water-colours.

The Spanish school is undoubtedly the most important and complete of all, especially in painters of the 16th and 17th centuries: **Morales, Gallego, Juan de Juanes, El Greco, Maino, Sánchez Coello, Zurbarán, Ribera, Murillo, Ribalta, Carreño de Miranda, Rizi, Valdés Leal, Alonso Cano, Goya** and **Velázquez.** The best represented are the last two.

Next comes the Italian school, with excellent works by **Mantegna, Botticelli, Fra Angelico, Raphael, Titian, Veronese, Correggio, Tintoretto, Bassano, Luini, Lotto, A. del Sarto, Giorgione, Lucca Giordano** and **Tiepolo,** very complete as regards range artists and number of works, especially by **Titian, Veronese** and **Tintoretto.**

The Flemish, German and Dutch schools are magnificently represented: **Hans Memling, Dürer, Rubens, Van Dyck, Jordaens, Teniers, Rembrandt** and **Antonio Moro.**

British, Swedish and Portuguese painting is hardly represented. The French school offers a good representative selection, with the names of **Watteau, Poussin, «Le Lorrain», Jean de Boulogne, Mignard, Simon, Vouet,** etc.

Sculpture is allotted a section to itself, though one or two pieces are distributed throughout the building in general.

Of great importance also is the lower-floor room devoted to the *Tesoro del Delfín*, where the jewels are on show which Philip V inherited from his father the Dauphin, son of Louis XIV.

There is also a very good collection of furniture,

tapestry, ceramics, coins and miniatures of different periods, donated by their owners to the Gallery.

The collection of drawings by **Francisco de Goya** is of the greatest interest; some of these are shown on the lower floor.

After this brief general survey, which is no more than the frame that outlines a picture, let us enter this great temple of Fine Art.

El Greco, Velázquez, Murillo, Titian, Rubens and **Goya** await us in the Prado to welcome us as hosts to their own house, to make us share their emotions and show us their art to the best advantage. Let us go in, even if only for an hour or two, on one of these pleasant Madrid mornings, and let us go back again as often as the length of our stay will allow.

In this little book, kind reader, I shall try to be brief, and to give you simple and definite information, arranged as clearly as possible. Let me guide you in this joint visit we are making. Later, in time to come, if you will take me down from your bookshelf at home, where I stand, maybe amid other reminiscences of a stay in Madrid, I shall bring back to your mind those hours when I was your guide, and you will remember the pleasures of that visit and the emotions those wonderful pictures aroused in you.

We meet, then, at the agreed hour, outside the doors, at the foot of that staircase facing the Calle de Felipe IV, with the statue of Goya before us. This is the best place from which to start.

We ascend the broad steps together to the main floor. Here is the doorway; we pass through it, and through the turnstile beyond, and we are in the Prado Gallery.

NOTE

To make this guide easier to use during visits to the Gallery, each page is headed by Roman figures denoting the number or numbers of the Rooms which it deals with. The Rooms follow one another in numerical order; those having the letter A after the numeral are new Rooms and are given immediately after the old-established ones bearing the same numeral without that letter.

Exceptions to this rule are the El Greco Rooms (X, XI and XXX) which go together, and Room X A which comes before Room X.

Thus the reader, whatever Room he may be in, can find the description of its pictures by simply turning the pages while looking at the Roman numeral at the top.

These pictures have been described in the places they occupied the moment of doing this guide, went to press. But the reader must not surprised if some have changed places since, for this is apt to occur in any art gallery in the world.

THE PUBLISHERS.

INTERIOR OF THE PRADO
MAIN FLOOR

ROOM I.—ROTUNDA. HISTORICAL PICTURES

Our pulse quickens as we stand before this sumptuous circular vestibule, surrounded by eight graceful Ionic columns, and giving a fine view down the central gallery.

But first we must greet the victorious Charles V, who awaits us in the centre of the vestibule: a bronze sculpture by **Leoni,** of eminently Renaissance characteristics; it has the interesting feature that the king's breastplate is removable, displaying a nude torso of magnificent proportions. The statue shows the Emperor Charles V victorious in his battles against the enemies of the Catholic Religion.

The walls of this vestibule are adorned by several historical paintings of the twelve that Philip IV commisioned for the Buen Retiro Palace; nearly all refer to Spanish victories in the Thirty Years War. They are large compositions in oils, with a plethora of narrative details; some have been badly restored.

N.º **635,** *The battle of Fleurus;* N.º **636,** *Relief of the town of Constanza* by **Vicente Carducho** (1576-1638).

N.º **183,** *Capture of a stronghold,* by **Lucca Giordano** (known in Spain as **Lucas Jordán**) (1632-1705).

N.º **653,** *Recapture of San Juan de Puerto Rico,* D. Juan de Haro repulsing the Dutch, and N.º **654,** *Recapture of the island of St. Kitts,* by the brush of **E. Caxés** (1577-1634).

N.º **166,** *The prudent Abigail* by **Giordano.**

All these works belong to the Spanish School.

In other rooms, which we shall visit later, there are three more of this same series, namely: *The relief of Genoa by the Marquess of Santa Cruz,* by **Pereda;** *The recovery of the bay of Bahia de Brazil,* by **Maino,** and *The surrender of Breda,* otherwise known as *The lances,* by **Velázquez.**

In this vestibule or rotunda three doors are to be seen: a central one which leads to the Great Gallery devoted to Spanish painting, one on the right leading to the rooms devoted to Flemish painters of the 16th century, and a door on the left, which is the most convenient for an orderly tour, and leads us to the Italian paintings.

ROOM II.—ITALIAN PAINTING. RAPHAEL

After a long series of primitives, Italian painting reaches its maturity in the 16th century. The supreme aspiration of the artist of that period was a classical ideal; but not only art but culture also tried to restore antiquity and return to the Graeco-Roman world. Beside Saints and Virgins the gods and goddesses of paganism appear in unconcerned nudity; later, we find Christian Virgins clad in the opulent fleshly envelope of Venuses; perfection in form is achieved, and the sense of the nude is fully attained by a group of artists.

The course of this painting develops in the classicist style known as Renaissance, which was destined to become so widespread and influential throughout Europe, and within which there soon emerged groups or schools having well-defined features of their own: the Florentine school, which attained its highest perfection in drawing and is headed by **Raphael,** and the Venetian, led by **Titian,** in which high perfection in colour is to be observed.

Raffaele Sanzio (1483-1520), the world-famous painter who was head of this school, wich had repercussions throughout Europe. **Raphael,** a pupil of **Perugino** and later influenced by **Michael Angelo,** drew teachings from both. His life was very short, for he died at 37, but he left a vast legacy of work of genius, filled with a highly personal style of real grandeur. **Raphael** knew his craft to perfection; he was equally a master of fresco and oil, he had a great power of adaptation, and he painted in every minute detail, sometimes to the extent of actual miniature work.

Let us first look at the **N.º 299,** *Portrait of the Cardinal* (Plate I), painted on wood about 1510 and bought by Charles IV; the subject has been doubtfully identified as either Goulio de Medici, Dovizi di Bibbiena or Matias Schinners. The figure is half-length, a masterpiece in portrait painting, in which we can observe the true type of Renaissance prelate, with a face full of expressive power: one of those Princes of the Church, concentrated, keen and intelligent in his gaze; a portrait of extraordinary merit, both in drawing and colouring.

N.º 296, *The Holy Family and the Lamb*, date 1504; this was kept in the Virgin's robing-chamber at the Escorial, whence it was brought to the Prado in 1837.

It is one of the smallest panels here, lovely in its drawing
and delightful in colour, and we can perhaps see, in its
composition, some influences of **Fra Bartolomeo** or
Leonardo da Vinci.

N.º **302,** *The Virgin of the Rose*, painted about 1518,
also from the Escorial and closely related to the *Petit
Sainte Famille* in the Louvre. A picture of eminently
Raphaelesque technique for its composition, colouring,
and the grace of these lovely Madonnas, virgin-mothers
of classic profile, full of tendernss, with those delightful
children which move in their arms.

N.º **301,** *The Holy Family*, commonly called *The Pearl*,
which belonged to Charles I and Philip IV, who, on
seeing it for the first time, exclaimed, «That is the pearl
of all my pictures», whence its name.

N.º **298,** *Fall on the road to Calvary*, also transferred
to canvas in Paris, in 1818, signed by the author, date
about 1517; it was formerly in the convent of Santa
Maria dello Spasimo, which gave rise to the ridiculous
name of *El pasmo de Sicilia*. This work was sent by the
Viceroy Count Ayala to Philip IV, and was kept for
some time in the Palace and regarded as a very valuable picture, though not so utterly priceless as was formerly believed. The origin of the composition appears
to be the *Passions* of **Dürer.** Here we note the skilful
hand of a pupil, though the picture has great qualities of expressiveness in the attitudes and faces of the
figures that accompany Our Lord; the arrangement of
the figures also shows perfect drawing and a certain
classical grace, but rather poor in colouring.

N.º **303,** *The Holy Family of the Oak*, done about
1518, of which another copy with one or two variations exists in the Pitti Palace at Florence; painted by
Raphael with the assistance of one of his pupils. Also on show are several copies of works by **Raphael,**

of lesser interest, executed by his pupils and imitators.

N.º 300, *The Visitation*, bought by Philip IV for the Escorial in 1655. First painted on wood, it was transferred to canvas; although by the painter's own hand, we can notice touches by one of his pupils, perhaps **Perino del Vaga.**

N.º 297, *The Virgin of the Fish*, which we may date as 1513, during the painter's best period, was mostly done by **Raphael,** in collaboration with one of his pupils. It is a picture of surprising beauty, delicate and admirable in all respects.

N.º 304, *Andrea Navagero*, portrait of a Venetian writer and diplomat, a copy of the original in the Doria Gallery in Rome.

N.º 315, *The Transfiguration of Our Lord*, a copy, attributed to **Penni,** of the one in the Vatican Museum.

ROOM III.—FRA ANGELICO
AND BOTTICELLI

The gem in this room is **N.º 15,** *The Annunciation*, by **Guido di Pietro da Mugello,** better known as **Fra Angelico** (1387-1455), painted on wood in tempera, as a bench or predella, with scenes from the life of the Virgin. It was executed about 1445 for the convent of Santo Domenico at Fiesole and then acquired by the Duke of Lerma; later it was in the convent of the Descalzas Reales in Madrid until it came to the Prado. Three similar copies of the same picture exist in San Marco at Florence. A work of divine simplicity, with a surprising minuteness of detail, which reflects the stainless purity of a soul filled with spirituality; the supernatural, angelic element in this art, which uses no more form than is essential. It is a picture that comes forth from

the heart like a prayer; its figures, traced in smooth
and delicate lines, are of the finest Florentine art; the
whole is enveloped in luminous, limpid colouring, «knea-
ded with the light of Paradise», as Denis said. A prodigious work, displaying an art divine rather than purest
and matchless blue. **Fra Angelico** and **Massacio** are
the axes on which the painting of the day turned, and
are the twin peaks of Florentine painting.

N.º **577,** *Virgin and Child*, panel painted *al fresco* by
Antoniazzo Romano (1461-1508).

The Story of Nastagio Degli Onesti, three elongated
panels by **Sandro Botticelli,** of the Florentine school
(1445-1510), a pupil of **Filippo Lippi,** in which the
eighth novel of the fifth day of Boccacio's *Decameron* is
given in a series of four such panels, only three being
shown here. They were done in 1487 and are not their
author's best work; the drawing, while possessing **Botticelli's** own grace and vivacity, sometimes suffers from
excessive affectation. They have passed through several
collectors' hands. One of them remained in London,
and the three here shown were bought in Berlin by
Sr. Cambó, who donated them to the Prado.

This painter's work is very personal; his composition,
notable, with striking colours, and some errors of structure
in the drawing of his figures, which are always tasteful
and full of gracefulness. **Sandro Botticelli** coincides
with the peak period of Florence, and in his art we see
his characteristic notes of grace, lightness and vivacity
maintained in a line half-way between the refinement
of the Medici court and the Franciscan austerities preached
by Savonarola.

Picture 1, **N.º 2838.** Nastagio *(first scene to the left)*,
scorned by his beloved, parades his misfortune cres-
tfallen, thinking of suicide. A woman's cries startle him,
and he sees *(scene I)* running towards him a beautiful

girl, naked and with dishevelled hair, harried by mastiffs and pursued by a knight who threatens, sword in hand, to kill her. Nastagio seeks to defend her with boughs of a tree in lieu of weapons, but the knight bids him halt, and explains what he is seeing. He too, like Nastagio now, once loved this woman passionately, and when he could not bear her slights he committed suicide, thus damning himself eternally. When she died she was also damned, and since then the two of them have been suffering the punishment he sees, which is repeated every Friday, when they come out of hell.

Picture 2, **N.º 2839.** The knight pursues her whom he once loved so much, as he would a mortal enemy; he overtakes her and tears out her heart, which he throws to the dog *(scene I)*. But she immediately comes to life again and the pursuit is renewed *(scene II, at rear)*, and the punishment is repeated throughout all eternity.

Picture 3, **N.º 2840.** Nastagio, deeply moved, compares this with his own case and determines to teach his mistress a lesson; for this purpose he invites her and her relations to a banquet at the place of the vision. During the feast the apparition takes place, causing alarm among the guests, who want to protect the fugitive; but Nastagio stops them, while the knight in the vision explains what is occurring. Nastagio's beloved is so impressed that she repents and gives him her love.

N.º 143, *St. Jerome, St. Margaret and St. Francis*, all three standing, with a landscape background, by **Giacomo** and **Giulio de Francia,** two brothers who lived between 1486 and 1540.

ROOM IV.—PRE-RENAISSANCE ITALIAN PAINTING

N.º **2843,** *Angel musician.* Panel painted in fresco by **Melozzo da Forli** (1438-1494), which has some resemblance to other angelic figures in the Vatican Gallery.

N.ᵒˢ **2841** y **2842.** Two panels with scenes from the life of St. Eloy, atributed to **Tadeo Gaddi** (1300-1366), a pupil of **Giotto.**

Next, an elongated panel, **N.º 2844,** by **Giovanni dal Ponte,** a Florentine artist who lived from 1376 to 1437. It is an allegorical representation of *The seven liberal arts*, showing them accompanied by sages: Astronomy, with Ptolemy; Geometry, with Euclid; Arithmetic, with Pythagoras; Music, with Tubal-Cain; Rhetoric, with Cicero; Grammar, with Donatus; and Dialectic, with Aristotle.

N.º **244,** *The Virgin and St. Joseph worshipping the Child,* by **Maineri.**

But the best and most important thing in the whole room is a little oil painting, of such small size that its hardly catches the visitor's eye:

Above this picture hangs **N.º 577 a,** a triptych which when closed shows St. John the Evangelist and St. Columba, and when open, a head-and-shoulders of Christ between St. John the Baptist and St. Peter, by **Antoniazzo Romano.**

N.º **525,** *The Continence of Scipio,* somewhat doubtfully attributed to **Peruzzi** (1481-1536).

N.º **248,** *The Transitus of the Virgin* (Plate II), painted in 1462 or 1492 by **Andrea Mantegna** (1432-1506); a dry, precise work, with the hard tones of an engraving and no attractions of colour, but all perfectly measured and studied. In this work **Mantegna** reveals a fine observation of plastic forms, with naturalistic drawing and an admirable touch of the brush, as we observe in the small background landscape, sometimes a trifle harsh, but technically always supremely finished and perfect.

N.º **524,** *The Rape of the Sabines.*

N.º **477,** *The Virgin, the Child and two angels,* by **Francesco Rossi «il Salviati»** (1510-1563), from the Isabel de Farnesio collection.

N.º **287,** *The Holy Family,* by **J. Carucci «il Pontorno»** (1494-1557).

ROOM V.—PAINTERS OF THE ITALIAN RENAISSANCE

Here in the first place we have several pictures by **Andrea del Sarto** (1486-1531), a Florentine master of composition and drawing:

N.º **332,** *Lucrezia di Baccio del Fede* (Plate 1). These last two pictures are the best and reveal the painter's talents fully: perfect draughtsmanship and delicate colouring after the manner of illumination, and composition and distribution which are always perfect.

The room has another picture of his, N.º **112,** *The Virgin, the Child Jesus and St. John,* rather better than the foregoing, which belonged to the collection of Isabel de Farnesio.

N.º **111,** *Noli me tangere* (Plate 2), one of the best-known works of **Correggio** (1493-1534), date about 1525, a gift of the Duke of Medina de las Torres to Philip IV, who sent it to the Escorial, whence it came here. It shows Christ in the garb of a gardener at the moment of His appearance to Mary Magdalene. Here

we have a figure of Jesus that is affected and overbeauti-
ful; it is one of those soft, sweet, sentimental pictures.
It looks more like a pagan than a religious theme; the
colouring is very much like that of a pretty chromolitho-
graph. In this painting **Correggio** displays himself to
us in a theatrical attitude as the painter of a voluptuous
intoxication with beauty.

N.º **5,** *Don García de Médicis,* a child portrait by **Bronzino** (1513-1572), a mediocre work by this fine Italian
portraitist.

N.º **504,** *La Gioconda,* copy on panel in oil, of perfect characteristics as regards colouring and drawing of
the portrait of Monna Lisa in the Louvre. This was
perhaps painted by **Yáñez de la Almedina,** a Spanish
pupil of **Leonardo da Vinci,** who introduced the Renaissance forms into Spain.

N.º **338,** *The Virgin, the Child, St. John and two angels;*
and the charming portrait of the painter's wife.

N.º **243,** *Salome receiving the head of the Baptist,* by
Bernardino Luini (1480-?-1532), a supposed pupil of
Laonardo da Vinci, whose influence can be seen in the
sometimes mannered technique, based on an ideal of calm
gentle beauty, ingenuous and somewhat monotonous.

N.º **336,** *The sacrifice of Isaac stayed by an angel;* N.º **337,**
The Virgin and the Child Jesus; N.º **335,** *The Holy Family;*
N.º **579,** *St. John the Baptist with the lamb;* N.º **334,** *Mystical
theme,* the Virgin, the Child, a saint and an angel.

N.º **241,** *Jesus and St. John embracing,* is a copy of this
painter.

N.º **242,** *The Holy Family.*

N.º **522,** *The Annunciation,* by **Danielle de Volterra**
(1509-1566).

El Cardenal.—The Cardinal.—Le Cardinal.—Der Kardinal.—Il Cardinale

El tránsito de la Virgen.—The Death of the Virgin.—La dormition de la Vierge.—De Tod der heiligen Jungfrau.—L'Assunzione della Madonna.

ROOM VI.—ITALIAN PAINTING (Continued.)

In this room we meet with a series of important works by master of the Venetian group. They may serve as an introduction to the plenitude of the Venetian School which we shall admire later:

Two portraits by **Parmigiannino** (1503-1540), sober and well drawn: **N.º 279,** *Pedro María Rossi, Count of San Segundo*, and **N.º 280,** *Lady with three children*, painted between 1523 and 1527.

N.º 323, *Noli me tangere*, the drawing attributed to **J. Romano** (1499-1546) and the execution to **G. Penni «il Fattore»** (1488-1528).

N.º 69, *Alfonso II de Este* (?), a work attributed to **G. Carpi** (1501-1556), by to some; by others, to **Bronzino** (1503-1572).

N.º 329, *The Holy Family*, by **Jacopo del Conte,** a Florentine painter (1510-1598).

N.º 16, *Pietro Maria, physician of Cremona*, by the paintress **Luccia Anguisciola** (1538?-1565).

N.º 57, *The Scourging*, a panel first attributed to **Michael Angelo** and later to **Gaspar Becerra;** according to Venturi, it is by **Marcello Venusti** (1515?-1579).

N.º 283, *The Holy Family with an angel*, by **«IL Parmigiannino»** (1503-1540), very similar to another in the Uffizi Gallery.

N.º 18, *The Nativity*, by **Barocci** (1526-1612), purchased by Charles IV.

Numberless, *Christ on the Cross*, by **Barocci.** Left by the Duke of Urbino to King Philip IV, in 1628.

In the middle of the room is an Italian marble bust, *Christ with purple mantle*, later 16th century, donated by Mr. Harris.

ROOM VII.—VENETIAN SCHOOL

At the outset of the 16th century, Venice was the focus of a new tendency in art; the features of this were magnificence of luminosity which is expressed in richness of colouring, and freedom in the general assembly of compositions. The brilliant life of the Venetians was illuminated by art; Biblical scenes were painted in series of great artistic merit, and the beauty of the saints reveals their supra-terrene nature; even the figure of the Virgin appears clad in the beauty of the women of Venice. The Venetian painters are painters of light, who express their animic states less in drawing than in colouring, whose chromatic richness they reproduce with all luminosity. **Tiziano Vecelio** (1477-1576) was the firts and chief of this school. Endowed with a great artistic temperament from his youth, his great talents for painting were not long in making their appearance; he studied under **G. Bellini** and made rapid progress; on the death of **Giorgione,** the work of **Titian** was at its height, and he was now the painter of the Venetian aristocracy. Great lords, dukes, popes and kings were his clients. **Titian** was at the peak of his power, and was the possessor of a technique without the austerity or mysticism of the primitives, nor the decadence of his own successors. **Titian** is the representative of a balanced, perfect art, which gives equally intense joy to the senses and the mind, and whose most glorious purpose was to exalt nature in all its human vibration.

Endowed with a fascinating, exuberant vitalism, after a first period of imitation of **Giorgione,** his powerful vitalism is seen through colour. His long, busy life produced countless works; Charles V and Philip II heaped honours and favours upon him, thanks to which the Prado Gallery is able to show a selection of this painter's best and most important works. In Rooms VIII and IX we shall study him anew, for the best of his work hangs there.

N.º **448,** St. Jerome, penitent, is attributed to **Lotto** (1480-1556), a painter of the greatest delicacy and a personal interpreter of the Venetian transition period.

N.º **240,** Micer Marsilio and his wife, also by **Lotto.** More than half-length figures, between which a cherub is smiling maliciously. Was acquired at the meeting of **Rubens'** executors, then passed into the Royal Collections, and finally to the Prado.

The following works by this great painter hang here: N.º **443,** Our Lady of Dolours, a replica of N.º **444,** painted on wood. N.º **434,** Mystical theme: The Virgin and Child with St. George and St. Catherine.

N.º **444,** Our Lady of Dolours (Plate 3), on marble, much better than N.º **443** in this same room. It is a half-length of the Virgin, clad in a blue mantle; her face displays an intense sorrow that stirs the heart, on which account, it is said, the Emperor held it in high regard.

N.º **442,** The Saviour, as the gardener, fragment of a picture which represented the appearance of the risen Christ to the Magdalene. Only the head and shoulders of Our Lord remain; the canvas was cut and arranged by **Navarrete «el Mudo»,** in accordance with the orders of Philip II.

N.º **20,** Christ giving the keys to St. Peter, by **Visenzo Catena** (1470-1521).

N.º **288,** The Virgin with the Child in arms, between St. Anthony of Padua and St. Roch, by **Giorgione** (1478-1510); unfinished. Its authorship gave rise to several disputes; perhaps the soundest view is that it is a juvenile work of the painter named. From the Monastery of El Escorial.

After this, we have **N.º 50,** The *Virgin and Child between two female Saints*, by **Giovanni Bellini** (1429-1516);

N.º 437, «*Ecce Homo*», painted on slate; another of the pictures Charles V had in the monastery of Yuste.

ROOM VII A.—PAOLO VERONESE

This room is chiefly devoted to **Paolo Cagliari,** who was born at Verona and on that account known as **Paolo Veronese** (1528-1588), and shows some of his best pictures. In his work Venetian sumptuousness found its last and greatest interpreter. He worked effortlessly with extraordinary facility of creation and unique fertility. **Veronese** pays primary attention to the decorative element, whose colouring is marked by a gentle shading off luminosity by the application of a fine silver grey.

N.º 490, *The Virgin, the Child, St. Lucy and a martyr*, a work of the studio of **Veronese.**

N.º 498, *The Magdalene, penitent*. Knee-length figure. Dated 1583.

N.º 497, *Martyrdom of St. Mennas*. Against a background of architecture, the saint is shown kneeling, surrounded by soldiers, and the executioner with the sword.

N.º 486, *Livia Colonna*, wife of Marcio Colonna, Duke of Zaragollo.

N.º 487, *Lavinia Vecellio*, portrait of the daughter of **Titian,** by **Veronese.**

N.º 491, *Jesus among the Doctors*, a canvas of large size, among the artist's best work, in which we see his addiction to the decorative element; against a background of columns and sumptuous palaces we see the figure of the youthful Jesus, the Doctors clad in the style of the

period, and on all sides the luxury, colour, and osten-
tatiousness of Venice, but all of it toned down and shaded
off by a greyish tint.

Lastly, **N.**º **406,** the portrait of *Paolo Cantareno*, by
anonymous Italian of the school of **Tintoretto.**

N.º **501,** *The Family of the wandering Cain*, of which
two other specimens exist in Vienna.

N.º **492,** *Jesus and the Centurion* (Plate 4), a work of
the painter's last period, bought by Philip IV at the
auction of Charles I of England; it was in the Escorial,
and was brought thence to the Prado in 1839.

In the picture **N.**º **499** entitled *The young man between
Virtue and Vice* we see his typical coloursoftening. A replica
of this work exists in the Frick Collection in New York.

N.º **270,** *The mystical betrothal of St. Catherine*, an
anonymous work of the Venetian school, with halflength
figures of the Virgin, the Child, St. Elizabeth, St. Joseph
and St. John.

ROOM VIII.—PICTURES BY TITIAN

N.º **446,** *St. Margaret*, a work from the studio of Titian.

N.º **447,** *St. Catherine*, from El Escorial.

N.º **439,** *Jesus and the Cyrenean*, a perfect picture full
of religious unction, in which the figure of Christ has a
moving expression.

N.º **430,** *Religion saved by Spain*, a canvas which he
repeated, with some variations, for the Doria family.
Was sent to Philip II after the battle of Lepanto.

N.º **438,** *Jesus and the Cyrenean*, a work similar but
inferior to **N.**º **439** in this same room.

N.º **533,** *The Elector Johann Friedrich, Duke of Saxony*.

N.º **431,** *Philip II, after the victory of Lepanto, offers*

Prince Fernando to heaven. The Prince was born two months
after the victory (1571) and died in 1578.

N.º **412,** *The gentleman with the watch,* which some
take to represent Juanelo Turriano.

N.º **414,** portrait of *Daniello Barbaro, patriarch of
Aquileya.*

N.º **420,** *Venus delighting in music* (Plate III), a picture
with one or two variants but similar to N.º **421** which
we shall see in Room IX. Here, the reclining goddess
amuses herself with a little dog; in the other, a cupid
appears. We may regard this work as belonging to the
painter's last period. It is a perfect study of the female
nude, with charming lines and really extraordinary flesh
tints.

N.º **413,** *The man with the ermine collar,* portrait of
an unidentified sitter.

ROOM VIII A.—VERONESE AND OTHER
MASTERS

N.º **374,** *A Venetian magistrate,* and N.º **370,** *A Jesuit,*
both by **Tintoretto.**

N.º **500,** *Abraham's sacrifice,* a late work by **Veronese.**

N.º **381,** *Self-portrait* of **Marietta Robusti,** daughter
of **Tintoretto.**

N.º **484,** *Young married lady,* doubtfully attributed
to **Tintoretto.**

N.º **479,** *Allegory: Birth of Prince Ferdinand, son of
Philip II,* by the Venetian painter **Michele Parrasio**
(1516-1578).

N.º **480,** *St. Agatha,* by **Carletto Veronese,** son of
Paolo.

N.º **483,** *Susanna and the Elders,* a juvenile work of
Veronese; he used this theme several times.

N.º 502, *Moses saved from the waters of the Nile* (Plate IV). Painted by **Veronese** in 1575; a small canvas of fine composition and colouring, with the curious anachronism that Pharaoh's daughter and her ladies are clad in the sumptuous dresses of contemporary Venice.

N.º 494, *The Marriage-feast at Cana*, by **Veronese,** a work of his first period, in which we observe the characters dressed in the height of Venetian fashion; beautiful ladies and 16th-century cavaliers attend the banquet, exquisite dishes are on the table, and there are columns and Renaissance elements in the background.

N.º 378, *The Gentleman with the Gold Chain.* A picture by **Tintoretto** which can be dated about 1550 and is regarded as one of the best portraits by this painter, to whom we are about to refer. Some take the sitter for **Paolo Veronese.**

N.º 482, *Venus and Adonis* (Plate 5). Painted by **Veronese** about 1580, a canvas with delicate silvergrey tones. Bought by **Velázquez** for Philip IV.

N.º 372, *Self-portrait* of **Paris Bordon** (1500-1570), an Italian painter.

ROOM IX.—TITIAN (Continued.)

This is one of the most sumptuous and best-conditioned rooms in the Gallery, devoted to the painter **Titian,** who, though not a Spaniard, enjoyed high favour from Kings Charles V and Philip II. In the first place, we have a collection of portraits of royal personages which is very complete and unique in the world. This series of works makes **Titian** the best represented of all Italian painters in the Prado.

As we enter, **N.º 415,** *The Empress Isabella of Portugal* (Plate 6), fine, delicate workmanship with great richness of colouring, and bearing witness to his extraordinary talent for portrait-painting; it was done at Augsburg in 1548, after the Queen's death.

N.º 419, *Offering to the Goddes of the Loves.* The statue of Venus in a flowering orchard. The field is thronged with winged Cupids, playing all sorts of games on the turf, as if to symbolize the various conditions of love, the feelings it inspires and the conflicting actions it gives rise to. This abode is approached by two suppliant nymphs, who, to propitiate the goddess, offer her a mirror and a votive tablet respectively; at the foot flows the spring of fertility or life; the theme is inspired by a passage in the *Eikones* of the sophist Philostratos. The picture was commissioned by the Duke of Ferrara in 1518, and afterwards copied by **Rubens,** with some variations, during his residence in Rome.

N.º 408, *Portrait of Federico Gonzaga, Duke of Mantua*, date about 1525, property of the Marquess of Leganés, from whom it passed to the royal collections and then to the Prado; a work of delicate quality, insuperable in technique and colouring.

N.º 409, *The Emperor Charles V*, aged between 30 and 40, with his favourite dog.

N.º 425, *Danaë receiving the rain of gold* (Plate 8). Jupiter, enamoured of the beautiful Danaë, enters her chamber metamorphosed into a rain of gold. A nude with fine colouring qualities, in which the figure of Danaë, with well-modelled body, is seen lying in an ecstatic trance upon the couch, while she receives the fecundating rain of the god. Of this «poem», which **Titian** painted for Philip II, there exists another copy in the Naples Gallery, clearly less fine than this one.

N.º 410, *The Emperor Charles V, on horseback, at Mühlberg* (Plate 7), a superb equestrian portrait, regarded by Frizzoni as the best in the world. The Emperor is shown

Lucrecia di Baccio del Fede

«Noli me tangere»

Lám. 2

La Dolorosa.—Our Lady of Dolours.—La Vierge des Douleurs.—Die
Schmerzensreiche.—La Dolorosa

Jesús y el Centurión.—Jesus and the Centurion.—Jésus et le Centurion.
Jesus und der Centaurier.—Gesù ed il Centurione

Venus y Adonis

La Emperatriz Doña Isabel de Portugal.—The Empress Isabella of Portugal.—L'Impératrice Isabelle de Portugal.—Das Bildnis der Kaiserin Elisabeth von Portugal.—L'Imperatrice Isabella del Portogallo

Carlos V

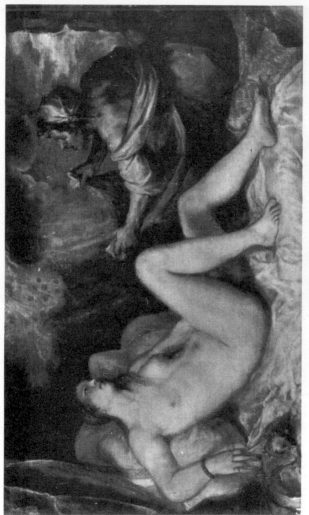

Dánae

Venus recreándose en la música.—Venus enjoying in music.—Venus et les plaisirs de la musique.
Venus mit dem Orgelspieler.—Venere mentre si ricrea con la musica

Moisés salvado de las aguas.—Moses saved from the Nile.—Moïse sauvé des eaux.—Die Auffindung Mosis.—Mosè salvato dalle acque

Bacanal.—Bacchanal.—Das Bacchanal.—Baccanale

Autorretrato.—Self-portrait.—Portrait par lui-même.—Selbstbildnis Autoritratto

Venus y Adonis

**La purificación de las vírgenes madianitas.—Madianite virgins.—Les
vierges madianites.—Die Madianitischen Jungfrauen.—La purificazione
delle vergini madianite**

El Caballero de la mano al pecho.—The gentleman with his hand at his chest.—Le geltilhomme de la main sur sa poitrine.—Der Edelmann mit der Hand auf der Brust.—Il Cavaliere dalla mano sul petto

La Coronación de la Virgen.—The Coronation of Our Lady.—Le Couronnement de la Vierge.—Die Krönung der Heligen Jungfrau.—L'Incoronazione della Madonna

**Adoración de los Pastores (detalle).—The Adoration of the Shepherds.
L'Adoration des bergers.—Die Anbetung der Hirten.—L'Adorazione
dei Pastori**

Don Julián Romero con San Luis, Rey de Francia.—D. Julián Romero
with St. Louis, King of France.—D. Julián Romero avec St. Louis, Roi
de France.—Der Hauptmann Julián Romero und der Heilige Ludwig,
König von Frankreich.—Don Julián Romero con S. Luigi, Re di Francia.

La Trinidad.—The Trinity.—La Trinité.—La Santissima Trinità

Cristo abrazado a la Cruz.—Christ embracing the Cross.—Le Christ avec la Croix.—Christus mit dem Kreuz.—Cristo abbracciato alla Croce

wearing the armour still preserved in the Royal Armoury
of Madrid; in his right hand, a lance, and in the background a landscape with the river Elbe. This represents
the moment when the Emperor rode out to do battle
against the Protestants in that famous engagement which
caused him so much anxiety. The picture came to Spain
among those belonging to Maria of Hungary.

N.º **421**, *Venus delighting in love and music*, similar to
N.º **420** in the preceding room.

N.º **411**, *Portrait of Philip II*, standing, full length;
shows the King as a young man, with his helmet on
a table. This picture of **Titian** was the one that Philip
sent to England so that his betrothed wife Mary Tudor
could know what he looked like.

N.º **428**, *Salome with the head of the Baptist.* In this
picture we have a fine portrait of the painter's daughter Lavinia, a girl of remarkable beauty, a true type
of Venetian womanhood, who sat for him on many
occasions; the work, dated 1550, is better than the other
copy in Berlin, wherein the head of St. John the Baptist
is replaced by fruit and flowers. The rich, sumptuous
colouring attests the exuberance and vigour of this celebrated painter's brush.

N.º **418**, *The Bacchanal* (Plate 9). Real identification
between pleasure and dignity, a work of extraordinary
merit, wherein we wonder which to admire most, the
marvellous grouping of the figures or the really por-
tentous colouring that the brush has given to the nude
torsos and the draperies of the figures, overflowing as
they are with profane, eminently Renaissance life. On
the right, in the foreground, the lovely Ariadne, asleep
on the grass, a youth and two Bacchantes, fauns and
young Bacchants; high up, on the right, a sleeping faun;
full-length figures which stand out from a background
of landscape.

N.º 407, *Self-portrait* (Plate 10), in which we see the painter, in old age, in profile and with the beard of a septuagenarian, with a calm expression and radiating his great personality; brought to the Prado in 1821.

N.º 445, *St. Margaret*, assigned to his last period.

N.º 440, *The Burial of Christ*, commissioned by Philip II in 1559 for the Royal Monastery of the Escorial. Of the two versions in the Prado, true, simple and artistic expressions of human grief, this appears to us the better; a similar one exists in the Louvre.

N.º 432, *Heaven*, a canvas of large size, which hung in Charles V's chamber until his death, after which it went to the Escorial, and thence to the Prado in 1837; it is apparently inspired by **Albert Dürer's** *The Trinity*.

N.º 422, *Venus and Adonis* (Plate 11), inspired by Ovid's poetical legend *Ars Amatoria*. It shows the goddess, who, in a foreboding of Adonis' death, clasps him in her arms at the moment when the young hunter is setting out with his hounds. We admire the Apollolike figure of Adonis, in contrast to the delicate beauty and finely delineated torso of the goddes.

N.º 429, *Adam and Eve*. Full-length figures perhaps inspired by those of **Dürer;** also a late work, in which we observe a warm colour toning and a perfect study of the nude.

In the corners of the room, on either side, are the bronze statues of Philip II and Maria of Hungary, sister of Charles V, by the Italian artists **Leone** and **Pompeyo Leoni**, father and son.

ROOM IX A.—TINTORETTO

Jacobo Robusti, commonly known as **Tintoretto,** also belongs to the Venetian school; a naturalistic painter who lived from 1518? to 1594, and who wrote his canon of perfection on his studio wall: «the drawing of Michael Angelo and the colouring of Titian». **Tintoretto** brought great dramatic power to the painting of History; a dynamic painter, with a forceful imagination which is manifested in the impetuous movement of his figures; a fiery artist who completed his works with speed and ease, with a bold, sweeping technique of motion. He felt stifled by the excessive cult of colour, and his own palette is one of broad, intense blotches, within a cold and audacious range.

In the first place the **N.º 2824,** *Washing of the Feet,* purchased by Philip IV at the auction of Charles I of England, and taken by **Velázquez** to the Escorial in 1656 together with other works. An oblong canvas of large size, of magnificent composition and figure distribution; in the background, a canal, with Venetian architectural details. Here already we notice his audacities in colouring; Father Santos said of this picture in 1657: «Here the great **Tintoretto** has a most excellent fancy in invention and execution», adding: «Hardly can the beholder be persuaded that it is painted; such is the power of the hues and arrangement in perspective, that the seems to be able to enter and walk upon the pavement within, and between the figures there is air, atmosphere».

N.º 391, *Judith and Holofernes.* The heroine is covering the beheaded body of Holofernes with a sheet, while her maid hides the severed head in a sack.

N.º 398, *Heaven.* Choirs of saints represent Heaven; below, the World. Purchased by **Velázquez** during his second trip to Italy.

N.º 394, *Visit of the Queen of Sheba to Solomon.*

N.º 382, *The lady baring her breast.* One of the most delicate and beautiful portraits by **Tintoretto;** some

suppose the sitter to have been his daughter, or perhaps
the courtesan Veronica Franco.

N.º **388,** *Esther before Ahasuerus.*

N.º **399,** *Battle between Turks and Christians,* a work
of lower artistic merit; N.º **367,** *Pietro de Medici* (?);
N.º **390,** *The death of Holofernes;* N.º **369,** *Archbishop Pedro;*
and N.º **371,** *A Venetian senator.* N.º **387,** *Prosperity driving
evils away,* a canvas attributed to **Domenico Tintoretto**
(1560-1635).

N.º **393,** *The Madianite virgins* (Plate 12). A picture done about 1570, which in itself sums up the essential
features of **Tintoretto's** art: boldness in drawing and
colouring, with a marked accentuation of greys and good
study of the nude in the figures. It was originally the
centre-piece of a ceiling, and surrounding it and comple-
ting the decoration were the following pictures in this
room: N.º **386,** *The chaste Susanna.*

N.º **389,** *Judith and Holofernes;* N.º **395,** *Joseph and
Potiphar's wife,* and N.º **396,** *Moses being taken out of the
Nile.*

N.º **397,** *The Baptism of Christ,* a picture of higher
quality than the one on the same theme in the church
of San Silvestre in Venice.

N.º **377,** *Portrait of an unknown person.*

ROOM X A.—THE BASSANOS

The **Bassanos** were a family dynasty of painters,
surnamed **da Ponte** and born at Bassano. They belong
to the Venetian school, and are as follows: **Francesco
«the Elder»** (15th century), **Giacomo** or **Jacobo,** son
of Francesco (1515-1592), and **Giacomo's** two sons
Francesco «the Younger» (1549-1592) and **Leandro**
(1557-1622). In this room there are several of their pic-

tures which are of much interest as a point of transition to the painting of **El Greco.**

The most important of the family is **Giacomo,** who specialized in Biblical themes. He matches colours well, and displays a concern for the problem of light. By him are the following: **N.º 25,** *The Adoration of the Shepherds;* **N.º 21,** *God's reproach to Adam;* **N.º 22,** *Entry of the animals into Noah's ark;* **N.º 32,** *Self-portrait,* and **N.º 26,** another *Adoration of the Shepherds.*

The following are by his son **Leandro N.º 41,** *The Crowning with thorns;* **N.º 39,** *The Return of the Prodigal Son;* **N.º 29,** *The rich man and Lazarus;* and **N.º 45,** *Magistrate or cleric with crucifix.*

There are some portraits by other painters: **N.º 366,** *A Venetian general;* **N.º 379,** *Venetian senator,* and **N.º 384,** *Marietta Robusti,* «*la Tintoretta*», daughter of the painter; all three by **Tintoretto.**

Finally, **N.º 380,** *Venetian senator,* by **Palma «the Younger»,** a member of the family of **Palma «the Elder»** (1544-1628).

On concluding our visit to this room, we proceed to the consecutive rooms numbered X, XI and XXX, to contemplate the Prado series of works by **El Greco.** For a fuller insight into his genius, a visit to Toledo is also recommended.

ROOM X.—EL GRECO

Domenico Theotocopulli, known as **El Greco** (1541-1614), came to Spain about 1577. We know that he was born in Crete, studied painting in Venice under the great **Titian,** and assimilated the best of **Tintoretto's** school. Perhaps as a result of some commission by Toledo Cathedral, or possibly attracted by Philip II's re-

putation as a great patron of artists, at any rate he appears
in Spain about that time. Philip II, however, did not
understand **El Greco's** painting, accustomed as he was
to the correct compositions of the Italians. Nevertheless,
El Greco removed to Toledo, where he spent the rest
of his life and developed his art, and where he found
the warmth and atmosphere appropriate for his work;
influenced by the passionately mystical spirit of the Spain
of that time, he fused himself into the spiritual climate
of 16th-century Spain and produced his works with a
fertility which astounds the world today.

His earlier pictures still show the influence of Venetian painting, with rich colouring and perfect drawing;
but his original temperament and technique rapidly
evolved in quest of solutions of his own.

Weary of Italian painting, with its repetitions and
mannerisms, its correct drawing and strident colours,
the painter emerges with a strong, original artistic personality.

His compositions seem to become concentrated and
simplified. He disregards beauty of form, abandons drawing, and turns out pictures of daring synthetic technique,
with splashes of colour, in quest of effects of light.

In his eagerness for expression and movement he
elongates his figures, dislocates their limbs and contorts
their bodies to the point of paroxysm; this is the moment
when **El Greco** has discovered mysticism, or rather,
mysticism has discovered **El Greco.**

Thereafter, his painting is steadily assayed and refined, his characters' faces are a faithful reflection of
his own inner life, and are as it were concentrated within
themselves; this inner life has the bitterness of time that
will not return and the longing for a higher world. His
brushwork is rapid; black, vermilion, ochre and white
form the essential key of his colouring, and accordingly

everything can be expressed with a greyish shading which characterizes his work. All this in conjunction gives **El Greco's** pictures their great personality.

A number of distorted and utterly nonsensical hypotheses have been invented about this great figure. Some have said he was a madman; others, a man of detective eyesight; but we can affirm, before all else, that he is a great artist, a painter of souls, a mystic.

El Greco is in painting what St. Teresa is or represents in the religious aspect. He had pupils, but created no school, and the fact is that only preeminent figures can rise to the limiting point he attained.

N.os **813** and **810,** *Portrait of an unknown gentleman;* **N.**o **827,** *The Annunciation,* a beautiful little picture of his first period; **N.**o **812,** *The Licentiate Jeronimo de Cevallos,* perhaps painted in 1608; **N.**o **2644,** *A Trinitarian or Dominican friar,* which was originally believed to be the painter Maino, and is classified as of his last period; **N.**o **811,** *Young gentleman,* and finally.

On either side, two half-length figures of saints: **N.**os **815** and **817,** *St. Anthony of Padua* and *St. Benedict.*

N.o **2445,** *Captain Julián Romero and St. Louis, king of France* (Plate 16).

Next come a series of perfect portraits: **N.**o **807,** *Doctor De la Fuente;* **N.**o **806,** *An unknowen gentleman;* **N.**o **809,** *The gentleman with his hand on his breast* (Plate 13), an authentic type of Toledan nobility, whom some identify with D. Juan de Silva, Marquess of Montemayor, notary of Toledo; the picture came from the country house of the Duke of Arco.

N.o **808,** *Don Rodrigo Vázquez,* president of the Councils of Finances and Castile.

ROOM XI.—EL GRECO (Continued.)

N.º 2890, *St. James the Greater,* which form part of an incomplete set of Apostles, of which we can see in this room the other canvases possessed by the Prado.

N.º 822, *Christ embracing the Cross* (Plate VI), a theme he repeated with one or two variants; signed; from the Museum of the Trinidad. Look at the touching expression of Jesus.

N.º 2892, *St. Paul;* **N.º 2891,** *St. Thomas;* **N.º 2444,** *St. John the Evangelist* (Plate VII), which was donated to the Prado in 1921; **unnumbered,** *St. Sebastian,* and **N.º 814,** *St. Paul,* more than halft-length, with a book in his hand.

N.º 826, *The Holy Family* (Plate VIII), in the same style as the one in the Hospital of Santa Cruz in Toledo; a theme he repeated on several occasions.

N.º 2889, *The Saviour* (Plate IX), **N.º 829,** *The Virgin Mary;* **N.º 820,** *St. John and St. Francis.*

N.º 2645, *The Coronation of the Virgin* (Plate 14), a work of his second period and a theme which he painted no less than four times. **N.º 2874,** *The Holy Face.*

ROOM XXX.—EL GRECO (Continued.)

N.º 823, *The Crucifixion,* a theme he repeated several times; origin of this canvas, unknown; date, between 1584 and 1594.

N.º 828, *Pentecost,* painted between 1604 and 1614.

N.º 825, *The Resurrection,* from the Museum of the Trinidad.

N.º 824, *The Holy Trinity* (Plate V), date about 1577, comes from the Convent of Santo Domingo el Antiguo

San Juan Evangelista.—St. John Evangelist.—St. Jean Evangeliste.—Der Evangelist Johannes.—S. Giovanni Evangelista

La Sagrada Familia.—The Holy Family.—La Sainte Famille.—Die heilige Familie.—La Sacra Famiglia

(Toledo); one of the first pictures painted by the artist after his arrival in Spain, with features in drawing and colouring that greatly remind us of the Italian masters; in particular we notice the influence of **Titian's** colouring.

N.º 2988, *The Adoration of the Shepherds* (Plates 15 and X), a work recently purchased by the Gallery and having magnificent qualities of light and colour, which markedly displays the sharp characteristics of the painter's spirituality in the expressions, attitudes and gestures of hands; it is regarded as a work of his last It formerly hung in the Toledo church of Santo Domingo el Antiguo, whence it was brought here.

N.º 819, *St. Francis of Assisi.*

N.º 2819, *St. Andrew and St. Francis,* from the Royal Monastery of the Encarnación in Madrid.

In one corner we see a sculpture of Christ bound to the pillar, by an anonymous artist of the 16th century, which goes perfectly with the art of **El Greco,** and two very interesting reliefs with themes from the Passion of Christ, of the same period.

The adjacent door brings us out into the Great Gallery of Spanish painting, and by the first door on the left, we enter.

N.º 821, *The Baptism of Christ,* a canvas done for the reredos of the church of Doña María de Aragón (Madrid).

ROOM XII.—VELAZQUEZ

Velázquez is the best painter of all time, and with **Goya** are the two best represented in the Prado. **Diego Velázquez de Silva** —perfect artist and serene observer—, was little given to fantasy or Baroque exuberance.

His works are regarded as a marvel of technique, for in them he gives a complete sensation of the volume and soul of things. From his earliest times he always painted his subjects from life, with hardly a trace of his masters' influences appearing; above all, he possesses an extraordinary personality, original and strong from the beginning.

He sincerely desired to paint things as they really are and not ideas; realism, truth, is his essential quality, to such a degree that his pictures seem like windows through which we look to contemplate the veracity of his themes.

He was born at Seville in 1599, and studied in the studio of **Pacheco** whose daughter he subsequently married. He later came to Madrid with a recommendation to his countryman the Count-Duke of Olivares, who protected him and introduced him into the Palace. Philip IV appointed him Court Painter, and thenceforth he was the favourite of kings and princes.

He lived in comfort and never knew the sufferings and misfortunes of the artists. He went to Italy twice, and his long artistic career was passed in the ambit of royalty. **Velázquez** was the painter of kings, and soon was to become the king of painters.

His calm, tempered art sought an objetive reality in things, such as no-one else has achieved; the dark notes in his colouring grow lighter until they reach those silvery shadings in greys so typical of him and called Velázquez greys.

He studied the effect of normal light on objects, until he attained the limit of subtlety and produced amazing results; in fact, he actually depicted light itself.

We shall briefly follow the pictoral evolution of this grand master in a series of works of the first importance.

If we start on the right as we enter this handsome

room, we shall first come to the portrait, **N.º 1188,** of *Prince Carlos*, brother of Philip IV, who is holding up a glove by one of its fingers. Painted about 1626-1627.

N.º 1171, *The forge of Vulcan* (Plate 17), finished in 1630 during his first visit to Rome. The mythological theme does not seem to have interested **Velázquez** much, for in reality it is a study of a number of male nudes, with highly expressive heads and faces.

N.º 1182, *Philip IV*. Perhaps the first full-length that **Velázquez** did of the king; about 1628.

N.º 1170, *The drunkards* or *Triumph of Bacchus* (Plate XI), a canvas painted about 1628, before his first trip to Italy, but in which we can notice some later modifications. **Velázquez** here gives us a skit on a mythological theme: a group of village boors indulging in the pleasures of wine and crowning themselves with vineleaves. The effects of the must are observable on their faces.

N.º 1181, *Don Gaspar de Guzmán, Count-Duke of Olivares* (Plate 18). A portrait inspired by the school of **Rubens.** Here this conceited and inept statesman of the court of Philip IV is parading as a valiant warrior.

N.º 1178, *Philip IV*. A large-sized equestrían portrait, in which the figure of the horse is oustanding; it is one of the best that **Velázquez** ever painted.

N.º 1208, *The god Mars*. A studio job, of little interest.

N.º 1185, *Philip IV*, rather more than head-and-shoulders; regarded as the best of all Velázquez' portraits of him. One observes the characteristic features of this king: phlegmatic face and prominent jaw and **N.º 1183,** Philip IV, half-length portrait, portion of a larger canvas.

N.º 1198, *Pablo de Valladolid* (Plate 19), the palace buffoon.

N.º 1180, *Prince Baltasar Carlos* (Plate XII). Equestrian portrait of Philip IV's son and heir, who died very young.

A canvas of delicate qualities depicting this charming child mounted on a spirited pony.

N.º 1200, *The buffoon called Don Juan de Austria.*

N.º 1172, *The surrender of Breda* or *The Lances* (Plate 20). A historical picture, and regarded as one of the best of this genre in Spanish art. It depicts the moment when General Ambrosio de Spínola, escorted by lancers, received the keys of the city of Breda from the hand of the defeated leader Justin of Nassau, who is followed by soldiers with lances and halberds, after the long siege of that stronghold. It was painted to adorn the Salón de Reinos in the Retiro Palace, where the rest of those in Room I (Entrance Rotunda) also hung. It is dated 1635 and is perfect in all respects, above all in colouring, which is no longer that of **Velázquez** first period, but has become more fluid, with finer tonalities, allowing grey transparencies to be seen.

N.º 1186, *Cardinal the Infante Don Fernando de Austria* (Plate 21), younger brother of Philip IV, in hunting dress, with a hound.

N.º 1191, *Queen Mariana de Austria* (Plate 22), niece and second wife of Philip IV, at the age of nineteen.

N.º 1184, *Philip IV* in hunting dress, with his favourite dog.

N.º 1193, *Don Juan Francisco Pimentel, 10th Count of Benavente* (Plate 23). Half-length. A typical nobleman of the 17th century, perfect in drawing and colouring; influences of **Titian** are observable.

N.º 1189, *Prince Baltasar Carlos* (Plate 24), in child's hunting kit, with harquebus and dogs; a marvel of infant charm. Observe the admirable blue-grey background scenery of El Pardo and the Guadarrama Mountains.

N.º 1194, *Juan Martínez Montañés* (Plate 25), the sculptor. Originally taken for Alonso Cano. A portion is unfinished.

N.º **1173,** *The Spinners* or *The Fable of Arachne* (Plate 26). The scene is the tapestry repair shop, which the Crown maintained for the royal service in the Calle de Santa Isabel and to which the painter must have been more tnan once. The theme is treated adequately, but what really arouses **Velázquez'** enthusiasm is the light and its action on the figures. Some figures receive the light direct, others remain hazy in penumbra; the figure with its back turned, stooping as if to pick up something off the floor, is hardly perceptible. In this picture everything is subordinated to the light, but a normal light, which is what determines its colouring. It is painted for effect and with a great sense of reality in thick strokes, which at a distance give a stereoscopic impression. It may be regarded as in the same line as the *Meninas*, which we shall see in Room XV. The date is about 1657 and it comes from the royal collection.

N.º **889,** *View of Saragossa*, done in collaboration with his pupil **Juan Bautista del Mazo.**

N.º **1192,** *The Infanta Margaret* (Plate XIII), a portrait of his last period, finished by his pupil **Mazo,** in which we see a marvellous technique in the combination of red and silver with the sumptuous whites and golden tones.

N.º **1206,** *Aesop* (Plate 27), and N.º **1207,** *Menippus*, burlesque interpretations of the celebrated fabulist and the Cynic philosopher; their date is about 1640.

N.º **1175,** *Mercury and Argos*, a mythological theme, very good in colour tonality, done in 1659 together with two others which were destroyed in the Palace fire of 1734.

Lastly, N.º **1199,** portrait of the buffoon *Barbarroja*, D. Cristóbal de Castañeda y Pernia, so nicknamed from his dressing in the Turkish style, painted in 1636 and left unfinished.

ROOM XIII.—VELAZQUEZ (Continued.)

In the middle of the Room is the interesting *Christ Crucified*, **N.º 1167,** dated 1628 and commissioned by the king for the Convent of San Plácido; after passing through several hands, it came into the possession of Ferdinand VII, who sent it to the Prado in 1829. We barely see the outline of the Cross itself; upon it, the naked body of Jesus dead, with bowed head and face almost covered by His hair. The modelling of the body is perfect, with hardy a touch of carmine. The whole is filled with a matchless serenity and beauty, sober and severe, without Baroque exaggerations or false pathetisms; it is the grave, majestic death of the Lord, one of the best and most beautiful pictures **Velázquez** ever painted.

To the right and left, **N.ᵒˢ 1220** and **1222,** praying portraits of *Philip IV* and *Doña Mariana de Austria, second wife of Philip IV*, which may be regarded as by some good pupil of **Velázquez.** They form a pair and perhaps adorned some Palace room.

N.º 1223, *Don Luis de Góngora y Argote*, the great Cordovan poet; this is a copy, the original is in Boston.

N.º 2873, *The Venerable Mother Jerónima de la Fuente*, a work of great power in drawing and colouring, from the Convent of Santa Isabel in Toledo. There is another copy in a Madrid private collection.

N.º 1209, *Francisco Pacheco*, portrait of Velázquez' master and father-in-law.

N.º 1166, *Adoration of the Magi* (Plate XIV). Also of his first period, dated 1617 or 1619. Nearly all the figures are portraits: some would identify the Virgin with the painter's wife, the young king with the painter, and the aged king with his father-in-law **Pacheco.** The work is full of dignity and notable qualities; we still see «tenebrist» influences, but we already observe the painting of types from life, possibly a little harsh in their outlines. The scene has real religious feeling, dignity and incomparable simplicity, and the Child Jesus in the Mother's lap is truly enchanting.

N.º 1224, *Self-portrait* (?), painted about 1623.

N.º 1195 and **1196**. Portraits of *Don Diego de Corral y Arellano, judge of the Supreme Council of Castile*, and his wife *Doña Antonia de Ipeñarrieta y Galdós with their son don Luis,* dated 1631; both veryinteresting and perfect, and classifiable as of his first period; donated by the Marquesa de Villahermosa.

N.º 2903, *Christ on the Cross,* signed in 1631, painted in grey tones with a technique like that of *The forge of Vulcan.*

N.º 1216 and **1217**. Two landscapes by **Martinez del Mazo** (1612-1667), **Velázquez'** son-in-law and one of his best pupils, a good painter who followed his master's technique and is notable for his excellent landscapes, though more still as a painter of superb portraits which are not eclipsed by those of the master and are sometimes confused with them.

ROOM XIV.—VELAZQUEZ (Continued.)

N.º 1179, *Queen Elizabeth of France,* wife of Philip IV. Equestrian portrait which hung in the Salón de Reinos of the Buen Retiro Palace.

Four portraits of buffoons, all perfect in their realistic line: **N.º 1201,** *El Primo;* **N.º 1202,** *Don Sebastián de Morra;* **N.º 1204,** *El Niño de Vallecas* (his name was Francisco Lezcano), and **N.º 1205,** *The buffoon Calabacillas, erroneously known as The Fool of Coria* (Plate 28), or Don Juan Calabazas.

N.º 1212, *The Arch of Titus at Rome,* attributed, with some reservations, to **Velázquez.**

N.º 1187, *Doña María de Austria, Queen of Hungary,* sister of Philip IV, who was courted by the Prince of Wales, later Charles I of England.

N.º 1197, *Doña Juana Pacheco,* Velázquez' wife.

N.ºˢ 1210 and **1211.** Two landscapes from the garden of the *Villa Médicis,* beautiful and perfect, in very modern technique, with impressionistic feautures, which he painted during his stay in Rome.

N.º 1169, *St. Anthony Abbot and St. Paul the Hermit,* painted to adorn the hermitage-chapel of St. Paul in the Buen Retiro. A raven is bringing the Saints their bread, while they are praying.

ROOM XIV A.—VELAZQUEZ (Continued.)

In this small transit room to the left we see **N.º 1203,** the *Buffoon Don Antonio «el Inglés».*

N.º 1168, *The Coronation of the Virgin* (Plate 29), a picture showing Italian influence, in which it is worth observing the noble face of the Virgin, beautiful and perfect, and the heads of the seraphs, wich are not inferior to those of **Murillo.** Painted for the Queen's oratory in the Madrid Royal Palace.

N.º 1219, *Philip IV armed, with a lion at his feet,* a work classified as of the studio of **Velázquez.**

Unnumbered, *Prince Baltasar Carlos,* a work of **Velázquez'** studio.

El Salvador.—The Saviour.—Le Sauveur.—Der Heiland.—Il Salvatore

La Adoración de los pastores.—Adoration of the shepherds.—L'Adoration des bergers.—Anbetung der Hirten.—L'Adorazione dei Pastori

ROOM XV.—VELAZQUEZ, LAS MENINAS

We now face picture **1174,** *The family of Philip IV*, commonly known as *Las Meninas* (Plate 30), a Portuguese word meaning little girls or maids. Princess Margarita plays with her court of little ladies, her dwarfs and her pet dog; in the centre, the little Infanta with two *meninas:* Doña María-Agustina Sarmiento, who is offering her a jug of water; while Doña Isabel de Velasco drops a graceful curtsey, to the right, the dwarf woman Maribárbola, with her deformed head, looks forwards, and Nicolasito Pertusato plays with the mastiff; all beneath the surveillance of the lady of the Palace D.ª Marcela de Ulloa, who is conversing with a gentleman.

Velázquez, before a canvas of which we see the back, is painting the King and Queen, whose figures can be seen reflected in the black-framed mirror on the back wall, while see gentleman in the distance passing through a helf-open door, lit by light from another room.

Space and light are indeed the real theme of this peerless work, the best that **Velázquez** ever painted. It is light that allots to each character the role it is to play in the picture; stronger on the foreground figures, and less on the rest, gradually fading, as they grow more distant, into the near-twilight of the dark corner of the room.

The colouring is extremely exact, in tonalities precisely proportioned to the light received, so that as we look at the picture we get a feeling of reality that almost invites us to walk into the canvas and join the scene.

This astounding work, regarded as one of the best in the Gallery, has been called «the theology of painting». No wonder Théophile Gautier exclaimed in surprise when he saw it, «Where is the picture?», since it looks more like a living scene, as we can prove still better if we look at it in the mirror which is in a corner of the room.

ROOM XVI.—RUBENS

Peter Paul Rubens, who was born at Siegen (Westphalia) in 1577, d. 1640, is the most authentic figure in the whole art of Flanders. A contemporary of **Velázquez,** he synthesizes the whole painting movement of Flanders which we shall now see. The genius of **Rubens** produced countless works to be seen in these galleries, side by side with those of his pupils, admirers and imitators. Some were painted in collaboration, and we cannot be sure where the master's hand stops and the pupil's begins. Let us take a glance at the chief pictures shown here.

Rubens was trained during a residence of eight years in Italy. His art is an emanation of exuberant naturalism, often vehement, full of intense high spirits, which he evokes with strong touches of colour. He goes in a great deal for mythological pieces, which is where his paganizing genius shines best. His pictures, golden and exact in colouring, show us marvellous nudes, which he introduces whenever possible amid great luxury and pomp of decoration. We may regard him as the best creator of mythologies after **Titian,** but we must also consider him as a painter of religious subjects in the service of the victorious Counter-Reformation. He was twice in Spain: in 1603 and in 1628.

We see disseminated in this room from **n.º 1646** to **n.º 1653** part of an incomplete set of Apostles, who are depicted half-length. This set was in the Royal Palace at Aranjuez.

N.º 1686, *Philip II on horseback.*

N.º 1639, *The Holy Family, with St. Anne.* Painted in 1626. The scene, whose great baroque naturalness is evident, is more human than divine. The features of the Virgin are reminiscent of those of Isabel Brandt, the painter's wife. The picture came to the Gallery from the Escorial in 1839.

N.º 1638, *The adoration of the Magis.* Painted in 1609 for the City Coporation of Antwerp. The Burgomaster presented it to don Rodrigo Calderón, and at the auction of his property after his execution, it was purchased by Philip IV. This large-size picture fully displays the essential features of the art of **Rubens:** his sumptuousness, colouring and drawing.

N.º 1643, *The Supper at Emmaus.* Painted about 1638.

N.º 1687, *Equestrian portrait of Prince Ferdinand of Austria, at the battle of Nordlingen,* with a Latin inscription recounting the incidents of the battle.

N.º 1642, *Pietà,* a very good work, with a perfect study of the body of Jesus, from the Monastery of El Escorial.

N.º 1644, *Fight of St. George with the dragon.* Purchased at the meeting of **Rubens'** executors.

Lastly, **N.º 1692,** *Adam and Eve,* a free copy from **Titian** by **Rubens,** made in Spain during his second visit.

ROOM XVI A.—VAN DYCK

Anton van Dyck, regarded as **Rubens'** best pupil, is one of the best portrait-painters of all time. He was born at Antwerp in 1599, and we may consider him the prototype of the gentleman, elegant and full of a natural distinction, which appears in all his work. His portraits are magnificent and most expressive; we note how he elongates the oval of the face and places the slender, elongated hands in the position of most advantage. He profiles the nose with perhaps more delicacy than any other painter has done. All the English portrait-painters of the 18th century follow him. **Van Dyck** is elegance in the portrait, the painter of chromatic exquisitenesses, handsome faces, gallant attitudes and slender hand.

N.º **1482,** *Frederick Henry de Nassau, Prince of Orange.*

N.º **1474,** *The Crowning with Thorns,* reminiscent of the «Ecce Homo» of **Titian.**

N.º **1485,** portrait of *Unknown woman;* N.º **1479,** *The painter Martin Rickaert,* who lacked his left hand; N.º **1490,** *The musician Enrique Liberti;* N.º **1477,** *The Arrest,* a picture of his first period, painted for **Rubens,** who esteemed it highly, and on whose death Philip IV bought it.

N.º **1481,** *Diana Cecil, Countess of Oxford;* from the Duque del Arco's country house.

N.º **1487,** *The musician Jacobo Gaultier* (?); N.º **1478,** *St. Francis of Asoisi;* N.º **1637,** *The brazen serpent,* attributed by some to **Rubens;** N.º **1480,** *Cardinal Prince Ferdinand of Austria;* N.º **1484,** *Charles I of England,* on horseback, in armour; he was in Madrid in 1623 while Prince of Wales.

N.º **1486,** *The Count of Bergh;* N.º **1492,** *Diana and Endymion surprised by a satyr,* painted about 1626. N.ᵒˢ **1491** and **1694,** head studies of an old man; the influence of his master is observable.

N.º **1489,** *Sir Endymion Porter and Van Dyck,* an oval picture showing them at halft-legth. This was done at the artist's best period and is considered one of his best portraits for its delicacy and elegance.

N.º **1488,** *The engraver Paul du Pont;* **N.º 1475,** *Pietà,* a beautiful picture, one of several he did on the same theme.

ROOM XVII.—RUBENS (Continued.)

N.º **1683,** *Archduke Albert of Austria;* **N.º 1688,** *St. Thomas More, Lord Chancellor of England,* copy of **Holbein** by **Rubens; N.º 1684,** *Princess Isabel Clara Eugenia.*

N.º **1991,** *Garland with Jesus and St. Teresa,* and **N.º 1994,** *Garland with the Virgin, the Child and St. John,* both by the Flemish paintress **Catharina Ykens** (1659-?).

N.º **1645,** *Act of devotion of Rudolf I of Hapsburg,* by **Rubens,** from the Royal Collections.

N.º **1685,** *Maria de' Medici, Queen of France* (Plate 31), wife of Henry IV *el Bearnés,* regarded as a fine portrait; **N.º 1418,** *The Virgin and Child surrounded by flowers and fruits,* painted in collaboration with **Brueghel. N.º 1689,** *Anne of Austria, queen of France,* sister of Philip IV and married to Louis XIII. Another copy of this exists.

N.º **1414,** *Cybele and the Seasons,* in a festoon of fruits, by **Brueghel** (1568-1625) and **Van Balen** (1575-1632); **N.º 1662,** *Atalanta and Meleager hunting the Calydonian boar,* painted by Rubens between 1639 and 1640; similar to the one in the Brussels Museum, and **N.º 1460,** *Garland with three loves,* by **Christian Lucks** or **Lycks** (1623-1653).

ROOM XVII A.—VAN DYCK AND JACOB JORDAENS

N.º **1545,** *The Child Jesus and St. John,* by **Jordaens** (1598-1678), a pupil of **Rubens** who followed his master's footsteps, but with less gracefulness and intensity. His pictures are lively in composition and nearly always very realistic, though without **Rubens'** richness of colour.

N.º **1661,** *Achilles discovered by Ulysses,* a work of collaboration between **Rubens** and **Van Dyck; N.º 1496,** *The Virgin of the Roses,* by a pupil of **Van Dyck.**

N.º **1546,** *Meleager and Atalanta,* painted about 1628 by **Jordaens.**

N.º **1550,** *Three itinerant musicians,* a small picture, whose drawing and liveliness of colour makes it look contemporary; it was long attributed to **Jordaens,** but a sounder view assigns it to **Van Dyck.**

N.º **1544,** *The mystical betrothal of St. Catherine of Alexandria,* regarded as by **Jordaens** though it has also been attributed to **Van Dyck** and **Rubens.**

N.º **1494,** *St. Rosalia,* and N.º **1495,** *Maria Ruthwen* the painter's wife, both by **Van Dyck.**

N.º **1549,** *The painter's family* (Plate 32), by **Jordaens,** a canvas regarded as his masterpiece. The gentleman with the lute is thought to be a self-portrait; his wife Catherine is the lady seated, followed by their daughter and a servant.

Next come some mythological pieces: **N.º 1547,** *Offering to Pomona,* perhaps one of the first pictures of **Jordaens,** and **N.º 1548,** *Goddesses and nymphs after bathing,* by the same.

N.º **1493,** *Doña Policena Spínola, marquesa de Leganés.* The daughter of Ambrosio Spínola, the victor of Breda. A very beautiful portrait, with a certain charm in the face and perfect drawing of the hands. Painted by **Van Dyck.**

ROOM XVIII.—RUBENS (Continued.)

N.º 1640, *Rest on the flight into Egypt;* **N.º 1666,** *Nymphs and satyrs,* purchased at the meeting of *Rubens'* executors; **N.º 1691,** *Dance of villagers,* a popular theme, done between 1636 and 1640; **N.º 2455,** *Achilles discovered by Ulysses,* and **N.º 2456,** *The rout of Sennacherib,* both in collaboration with **Van Tulden.**

N.º 1710, *Hercules and the hydra,* copy of **Rubens** by **Mazo; N.º 1665,** *Diana and her nymphs surprised by satyrs,* one of **Rubens'** masterpieces.

N.º 1725, *Diana the huntress,* from the studio of **Rubens.**

N.º 1690, *The garden of love,* a canvas painted about 1638, in which we recognize the painter in the gentleman on the right, and his wife Elena Fourment in the lady in the middle, who rests on the knee of the following one. The main part of the picture is **Rubens'** work; the scenery and other subsidiary details, by his pupils. It is one of his finest works, and shows the sensual exuberances to which he is given, in a series of nymphs, cupids, gentlemen and flowers which fill the canvas, overflowing with gaiety and the joy of living.

Lastly, **N.ᵒˢ 1420** and **1999** flower and fruit pieces.

ROOM XVIII A.—RUBENS (Continued.)

In this room hang the following mythological paintings: **N.º 1677,** *Mercury;* **N.º 1663,** *Andromeda freed by Perseus,* perhaps one of **Rubens'** last works, which has to be finished by **Jordaens; N.º 1681,** *Democritus, or the laughing philosopher;* **N.º 1674,** *Fortune.*

N.º **1670,** *The Three Graces,* a canvas painted about 1639 during the artist's best period; this is one of his capital works, of splendid colouring and sensual exuberance. The Three Graces, Aglaia, Euphrosyne and Thalia, standing, nude and with linked arms, against a background of landscape. The figure on the left was modelled by the painter's wife Elena Fourment.

N.º **1679,** *The rape of Ganymede,* painted to adorn the Tower of the Parada; N.º **1678,** *Saturn,* devouring one of his sons; N.º **1669,** *The Judgement of Paris,* a masterpiece of his and a theme he repeated several times, though this is the best.

N.º **1676,** *Vulcan forging the thunderbolts of Jupiter,* classified as a studio job; N.º **1682,** *Archimedes in meditation.*

Lastly, N.º **1680,** *Heraclitus, or the weeping philosopher.*

ROOM XIX.—RUBENS (Continued.)

This room contains some of the 17 sketches that Princess Isabel Clara Eugenia commissioned from **Rubens** for tapestries for the Madrid Convent of the Descalzas Reales: N.º **1700,** *The Triumph of the Divine Love;* N.º **1699,** *Triumph of the Eucharist over Idolatry;* N.º **1697,** *Triumph of the Catholic Truth;* N.º **1702,** *The four Evangelists;* N.º **1701,** *Triumph of the Eucharist over Philosophy;* N.º **1698,** *Triumph of the Church;* N.º **1695,** *St. Clara among Fathers and Doctors of the Church;* and **1696,** *Abraham offering the tithe to Melchisedech.*

N.º **2454,** *The education of Achilles,* and N.º **2566,** *Briseïs restored to Achilles,* both by **Rubens** in collaboration with **Van Tulden.**

Finally, several small pictures by **Rubens,** sketches on mythological themes.

Los Borrachos o El triunfo de Baco (fragmento).—The drunkards or Triumph of Bacchus.—Les ivrognes ou Le triomphe de Bacchus.—Bacchus und die Zechbrüder.—Gli Ubbriachi, od Il Trionfo di Bacco

El Príncipe Baltasar Carlos

ROOM XX.—RUBENS AND PUPILS

N.º **1693,** *The rape of Europa,* copy of **Titian** by **Rubens** during his second stay in Madrid.

N.º **1463,** *Jupiter and Lycaon,* by **J. Cossiers,** Flemish painter (1600-1671).

N.º **1671,** *Diana and Callisto,* by **Rubens,** in collaboration with pupils, N.º **1628,** *Rape of Europa,* by **Quellyn** (1607-1678).

N.º **1727,** *Diana's hunt,* by **Rubens** except for the dogs, attributed to **P. de Vos** (1596-1678). The Room also displays several pictures having flower-garland themes, all by painters of the same school.

ROOM XXI.—FLEMISH SCHOOL. P. DE VOS
AND J. COSSIERS

By **Paul de Vos** (1596-1678), a Fleming who specialized in animal and hunting and shooting pictures, we here see two broad canvases which he did for Philip IV: N.º **1870,** *Stag beset by hounds,* and N.º **1869,** *Roebuck hunt,* both giving a good study from nature. They come from the Royal Collections.

By **Jan Coetsiers** or **Cossiers** (1600-1671), a pupil of **Rubens** who was very fond of mythological subjects, we have N.º **1465,** *Narcissus looking at himself in the pool,* signed by the artist.

N.º **1673,** *Mercury and Argos,* from the studio of **Rubens,** with the collaboration of his pupil **Van Uden** (1595-1672).

N.º **1718,** *Love asleep,* also from the studio of **Rubens.**

Lastly, N.º **1672,** *The goddess Ceres and the god Pan,* by **Rubens** and **F. Snyders** (1579-1657), together with two flower-pieces attributed to **Brueghel.**

ROOM XXII.—DUTCH SCHOOL. REMBRANDT

Rembrandt (1606-1669) is the head of the so-called realist school of Holland. No-one showed such mastery of problems of light and shade, and he achieved marvellous effects. A lyrical painter, he puts all his feelings and passion into his pictures, and he is outstanding for his admirable colouring. In this room hangs **N.º 2808,** one excellent *Self-Portrait* out of the many he did during his life; it is thought to be between 1660 and 1663.

The room also contains works by the following painters:

By **Adriaen van Ostade** (1610-1684), a good painter and engraver, several amusing scenes of popular life: **N.º 2123,** *Villagers singing;* **N.ºˢ 2121** and **2126,** *Rustic concert;* **N.º 2122,** *Village kitchen,* and **N.ºˢ 2124,** *The five senses: Sight,* and **2125,** *The five senses: Hearing.* The last two are copies of lost originals.

By **Philips Wouwerman** (1619-1668), a painter very fond of hunting themes, we have **N.º 2150,** *Going out hawking;* **N.º 2151,** *Leaving the inn,* and some more on similar subjects.

By **Paulus Potter** (1625-1654): **N.º 2131,** *In the meadow,* two cows and a goat: **N.º 2097** *Offering,* by **P. F. Grebber** (1600-1653).

By **Gerard van Honthorst** (1590-1656), **N.º 2094,** *The unbielief of St. Thomas,* a well-painted canvas, in which we can clearly appreciate the imitation of the style of **Caravaggio.**

By **Gabriel Metsu** (1630-1667) **N.º 2103,** *Dead cock.*

Also a landscape by **Jan van Goyen** (1596-1656) and other works of lesser importance.

ROOM XXIII.—DUTCH PAINTING (Continued.)

N.º **1728,** *Wood,* and **1729,** *Landscape,* by **Ruysdael** (1628-1682), and between them *The philosopher,* by **Köninck; N.º 2586,** *Scene of soldies,* by **Palamedes** (1601-1673).

Also, **unnumbered,** *The Adoration of the Shepherds,* a work which bears the anagram of **Rembrandt** but is attributed to **Samuel Koninck; N.º 2149,** *Going out hawking,* and **N.º 2147,** *Going out hunting,* both by **Wouwerman.**

N.º **2860,** *Landscape,* by **Hobbema** (1638-1709); N.º **2133,** *The girl with the barrel,* a work by the school of **Rembrandt; N.º 2588,** *Young man with hand before his chest,* by **Van Ceulen; N.º 2154,** *Skirmish between Moors and Christians,* and **N.º 2152,** *Halt at the inn,* both by **Wouwerman.**

N.º **2132,** *Artemisa* (Plate 33), by **Rembrandt.** The queen of Pergamus receiving the ashes of her husband in a chalice, a work very typical of this artist, in which we note the interesting golden tones it is painted with the perfect study of the hands and the expressive drawing of the head. It is an allusion to faithfulness and conjugal love. Purchased in 1779 by the painter **Mengs** for the Marqués de la Ensenada.

Lastly, **N.º 2135,** *Light effect,* by **Schalcken** (1643-1706).

ROOM XXIV.—SPANISH PAINTING OF THE 15TH CENTURY

This room, adjoining the entrance Rotunda and vestibule of the central Great Gallery, is devoted to Spanish primitives, of whom the following works are hung:

N.º 705, *The Visitation;* **N.º 708,** *Baptism of Christ;* **N.º 706,** *Birth of St. John the Baptist;* **N.º 707,** *Preaching of St. John the Baptist,* and **N.º 710,** *Beheading of the Baptist* (Plate 34), and **N.º 709,** *Imprisonment of St. John the Baptist,* a collection of six panels by a **Hispano-Flemish anonymous painter** of the end of the 15th century. They come from the Charterhouse of Miraflores (Burgos), and were originally classified as of the school of **Fernando Gallego.**

Pedro Berruguete (1450?-1503), a Castilian painter, father of the sculptor Alonso Berruguete, here gives us a collection of ten panels with various scenes or subjects concerning the Dominican Order:

N.º 616, *St. Dominic Guzmán;* **N.º 615,** *Appearance of the Virgin to a community;* **N.º 609,** *St. Dominic and the Albigensians;* **N.º 610,** *St. Dominic raising a young man from the dead;* **N.º 618,** *Auto-da-fe presided over by St. Dominic;* **N.º 612,** *St. Peter Martyr in prayer* (Plate 35); **N.º 611,** *Sermon of St. Peter Martyr;* **N.º 613,** *Death of St. Peter Martyr;* **N.º 614,** *Tomb of St. Peter Martyr;* **N.º 617,** *St. Peter Martyr;* these ten panels originally formed two reredoses of altars devoted to St. Dominic Guzmán and St. Peter Martyr, in the Convent of Santo Tomás at Avila.

Of this series, **Berruguete's** hand is responsible for the panels entitled *Auto-da-fe, St. Dominic and the Albigensians,* and *St. Peter Martyr,* and in them we observe the

artistic qualities of this extraordinary painter, the best
of the Spanish primitives, with his special features of
sobriety and expressiveness.

In the others, both quality and colour are notably
less good, which betrays the hand of one of his pupil-
collaborators; in Lefort's view, that of a certain **Santos.**

There is also **N.º 1305,** *The trial by fire*, a repetition
of the theme of **N.º 609.** We must point put that **Pedro
Berruguete** was the first Spanish painter who went to
Italy, but he did not thereby lose his sober Castilian
character or his narrative conception; his pictures tends
towards observation from life, and against the Flemish
tradition, he uses gold and silver freely in the backgrounds
and in vestments and decoration. In isolated figures, **Berruguete** shows great mastery and ease, and in mass
themes with multitudes, we can already desery something of picaresque realism.

N.º 2647, *Christ in benediction* (Plate 36), by **Fernando
Gallego** (1440-1507), central panel of reredos from the
church of San Lorenzo at Toro (Zamora), which came
to the Prado in 1913; a very meritorious work, influenced
by the style of the **Van Eyck** brothers, and perhaps still
more so by **Bouts.** The figure of Christ is majestic and
severe, and the fall of the draperies perfect and well-
conceived; everything accords with the teachings of the
Flemish painters.

Next, two doors of a triptych or panels of a retable,
with four scenes of religious subjects: by a **Spanish
anonymous painter, N.º 2575,** *The Annunciation;* **N.º
2577,** *The Nativity;* **N.º 2578,** *The Death of the Virgin;*
N.º 2576, *The Marquess of Santillana in prayer;* from the
Benedictine monastery of Sopetrán (Guadalajara). In
these, we notice influences of **Van der Weyden** and
Memling.

N.º 1326, *St. Michael the Archangel,* by an **anony-**

mous Hispano-Flemish painter of about 1475, perhaps
J. Sánchez de Castro, purchased from the Hospital of
San Miguel at Zafra (Badajoz) and brought to the Gallery in 1924; a panel of marked Flemish influence, which
we may classify in the Andalusian group, as can be seen
in the drawing of the angels and the mastery of colour.

N.º **1260,** *The Virgin of the Catholic Sovereigns* (Plate 37), by an **anonymous Hispano-Fleming,** painted
on wood, from the Convent of Santo Tomás at Avila.
An essential piece of Spanish primitive painting, with
clear intonation and good arrangement of figures and
planes, it contains authentic portraits of Queen Isabella,
King Ferdinand, their children Doña Isabel, Queen of
Portugal, and Don Juan, the inquisitor Torquemada,
and Pedro Mártir de Anglería, the introducer of huma-
nism into Spain.

On either side of the above, N.ºˢ **2935** to **2938,** four
panels by **Juan de Flandes** *The raising of Lazarus, The
Prayer in the Garden, The Ascension* and *Pentecost,* the most
representative works of this painter of the Catholic Sovereigns.

Lastly, N.º **1323,** *St. Dominic of Silos,* by **Bartolomé
de Cárdenas Bermejo,** a painter born at Cordoba
in 1442 who is one of the most representative Spanish
primitives. It comes from a portion of an altarpiece
called the retable of Daroca, and shows the Saint vested
in pontificals, with mitre, crozier and book, and seated
on a throne. We note how well the figure is wrought, a
worthy example from one of the most powerful of the
Spanish primitive painters, possessing a deep knowledge
of his craft, and endowed with a truly Spanish feeling
which is manifest in all his works, side by side with more
or less Flemish influences; notable also are the majestic
attitude of the Saint, the vigour he possesses, the delicacy
of embroidery on his cope, and the filigraned background.

GREAT CENTRAL GALLERY

ROOM XXV.—SPANISH PAINTERS OF THE 16TH AND 17TH CENTURIES

Francisco Ribalta, born in Solsona (Lérida) (1555-1628), was a contemporary of **«Juan de Juanes»** and is thought to have been his pupil. In the history of painting he represents the first naturalistic reaction against the whole series of painters who repeated the Italian modes and mannerisms.

Ribalta was the first of the realists, to culminate in **Velázquez,** who broke with all this second-hand classicism continually repeated by Italian-trained painters. His magnificent studies of light and his simple technique display his robust temper and accredit him as a realistic painter, endowed with great dramatic power in religious painting.

It is true that **Caravaggio** in Italy also followed the same technique, but he had no contact or points of coincidence with **Ribalta.** The latter, by his own means like other painters, advanced towards naturalistic art, solely at the bidding of his own mental reaction.

N.º 2804, *Christ embracing St. Bernard* (Plate XV),
a work we may assing to the painter's last period, though
originally attributed to **Zurbarán,** was acquired for
the Prado in 1940. Here we observe an intense religious
dramatism, the whole having a warm colour and good
restrained, austere drawing; the Saint's habit somewhat
prefigures the white habits of **Zurbarán's** monks.

N.º 3044, *St. Jhon the Evangelist.* Wonderful panel
from the first period of this painter, exhibited for the
first time.

Juan Bautista Maino (1568-1649), a Spanish painter, born at Pastrana (Guadalajara) of Spanish parents,
but until recently regarded as having been an Italian.
A contemporary of **El Greco,** he lived and painted first
in Toledo and then in Madrid, as drawing-master to
the then Infante Philip IV. At Toledo, while still very
young, he entered the Convent of San Pedro Mártir.
He knew **El Greco** intimately and worked in the latter's
studio beside **Luis Tristán** and **El Greco's** son Jorge
Manuel. His figure, as yet little studied, shows interesting
aspects. It is very doubtful whether be should be regarded
as a pupil of **El Greco;** possibly the latter's influence
accounts for his attention to the problem of light and
shade, but he always solves this in his own way

In the picture **N.º 885,** *Recovery of Bahía de Brasil,*
painted to decorate the Salón de Reinos in the Retiro
Palace, one of the best historical pictures, we can observe
his talents for portraiture, besides sound arrangement
and distribution of figures and noteworthy colouring. It
depicts the homage paid to Philip IV by the citizens of
Bahía on the recapture of the town by the Spaniards.

N.º 886, *Adoration of the Magi* (Plate 38), signed by
the artist, comes from the Church of San Pedro Mártir in Toledo, where he took religious vows. It is one
of four which formed the chief reredos; a beautiful canvas,

**La Infanta Margarita.—The Infanta Margaret.—L'Infante Marguerite.
L'Infanta Margherita**

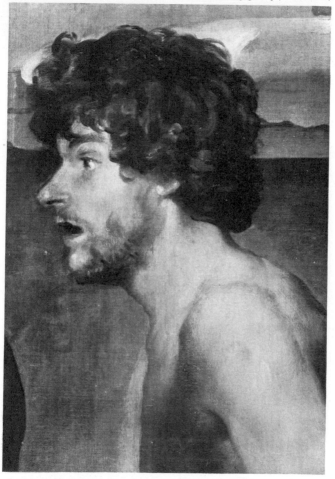

La fragua de Vulcano (fragmento).—Vulcan's Forge (fragment).—La forge de Vulcain.—Die Schmiede des Vulkan.—La fucina di Vulcano (frammento)

El Conde-Duque de Olivares.—The Count-Duke of Olivares.—Le Comte-Duc d'Olivares.—Der Herzog Graf von Olivares.—Il Conte-Duca di Olivares

Pablo de Valladolid

La rendición de Breda.—Surrender of Breda.—Reddition de Bréda.—Die Übergabe von Breda.—La resa di Breda

Retrato del Cardenal-Infante D. Fernando.—Portrait of the Cardinal-Infant D. Fernando.—Le Cardinal-Infant D. Fernando.—Der Cardinal-Infant D. Fernando.—Ritrato del Cardinale Infante D. Fernando

**Retrato de Doña Mariana de Austria.—Portrait of the Queen Mariana of
Austria.—La Reine Marianne d'Autriche.—Die Königin Marianne von
Österreich.—Ritratto di Marianna d'Austria**

**El Conde de Benavente.—The Count of Benavente.—Le Comte de Bena-
vente.—Der Graf von Benavente.—Il Conte di Benavente**

**El Príncipe Baltasar Carlos (detalle).—The Prince Balthazar Charles.
Le prince Balthazar Charles.—Der Prinz Don Balthasar Karl (Teilbild).
Il Principe Baldassarre Carlo**

Retrato de Martínez Montañés.—Martínez Montañés portrait.—Bild von Martínez Montañés.—Ritratto di Martínez Montañés

Las Hilanderas (detalle).—The Spinners.—Les Fileuses.—Die Spinnerinen (Teilbild).—Le filatrici

Esopo.—Aesop.—Esope.—Aesop.—Esopo

El bufón Calabacillas.—The Bufoon Calabacillas.—Le bouffon Calabacillas.—Der Hofnarr Calabacillas.—Il Buffone Calabacillas

La Coronación de la Virgen (detalle).—The Coronation of Our Lady.
Le Couronnement de la Vierge.—Die Krönung der Heiligen Jungfrau
(Teilbild).—L'Incoronazione della Madonna

Las Meninas (detalle).—The Meninas.—Les Menines.—Las Meninas (Teilbild).—Le «Meninas»

La Reina María de Médicis.—The Queen Mary of Medicis.—La Reine
Marie de Médicis.—Die Königin Maria von Medici.—La Regina Maria
de Medici

**La familia del pintor.—The Painter's Family.—La famille du Peintre.
Die Familie des Malers.—La Famiglia del Pittore**

Adoración de los Magos.—The Adoration of the Magi.—L'Adoration des
Mages.—Die Anbetung der Könige.—L'Adorazione dei Re Magi

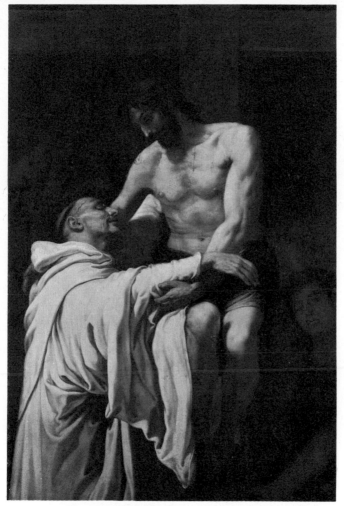

**Cristo abrazando a San Bernardo.—Christ embracing St.-Bernard.
Christ embrassant Saint Bernard.—Christus umarmt den hl. Bernhard.
Cristo abbracciato a S. Bernardo**

in a transition style, with gay forms and colours. **Maino** is an original, precise, naturalistic painter, with smooth colours having a certain fluidity and transparency that gives his pictures a truly delightful appearance; his style reminds us of the golden period of **Caravaggio.** He is much addicted to the study of light, but with a very rich colouring of his own, luminous and transparent, which makes this one of the most beautiful pictures on the subject in the Prado.

N.º **2502,** *St. Brune declines the archbishopric of Reggio*, by **Carducho.** On the left side of the picture we see Pope Urban II offering the archiepiscopal badges to the founder St. Brune, who puts them away.

N.º **3018,** *The Pentecost*, by **Maino.** In tight assembly we can see the Holy Virgin with another woman and the twelve Apostles looking at the Holy Spirit, who descends in fulgency upon them like a dove. St. John the Evangelist is dictating or perhaps reading The Acts of the Apostles. Panel painted in 1611 with destination to St. Peter Martyr's altar-piece in Toledo.

N.º **858,** *The surrender of Juliers*, by **José Leonardo** (1605-1656).

N.º **859,** *The capture of Brisach* by **José Leonardo** (1605-1656). (Spanish school).

N.º **1127,** Portrait of *A General of the Artillery*, by **Francisco Rizi** (1608-1685). (Spanish school).

N.º **639,** *The miracle of the waters*, by **Carducho.** On the background several temples are being to built up and on the foreground we see St. Brune and six of his disciples thanking God for the water flowing from the rock.

N.º **887,** *Don Tiburcio de Redín y Cruzat*. A full-lenght portrait of this Knight of Santiago, who took the Capuchin habit under the name of Francisco de Pamplona; a very delicate work, of a quality in portraiture capable of rivalling even **Velázquez.** Its classification was difficult at first, and for some time it was attributed to **Mazo,** but a fuller study confirmed it as the work of the Benedictine **Fray Juan Andrés Ricci,** or **Rizi de Guevara,** a Madrid painter who lived from 1600 to 1681.

Antonio de Pereda (1608-1678) was a Castilian painter of careful technique; **N.º 1317 A,** *Relief of Genoa by the Marquess of Santa Cruz.*

N.º 1340, *St. Peter Delivered by an Angel*, by **Antonio de Pereda.**

ROOM XXV A

This room is wholly devoted to painters of the Italian school. Here we meet in the first place **N.º 436,** with *The Prayer in the Garden of Gethsemane*, by **Titian.**

N.º 346, *The Descending of Christ into Limbo*, by the Italian **Sebastiano del Piombo** (1485 ?-1547), Venetian school.

Lastly, **N.º 345,** *Christ carrying the Cross*, by **Sebastiano del Piombo** (1485 ?-1547), date 1520. A well-executed work, with precise, vigorous drawing, and the theme deeply felt, with the influence of **Michael Angelo** observable; a replica of this is the Ermitage Gallery, part of the loot of art works from Spain by Marshal Soult.

N.º 2638, *The Virgin and Child*, by **Cima da Conegliano** (1460-1518).

N.º 417, *Address of the Marquess del Vasto to his troops*, purchased at the auction of the property of Charles I of England.

N.º 416, *The lady in the green turban*, attributed to **Dosso Dossi,** born at Ferrara between 1475 and 1479, died 1542.

N.º 441, *The burial of Christ,* a scene with variations on picture **N.º 440** which we shall see in Room IX.

N.º 452, *Philip II,* from Titian's atelier.

N.º 433, *The Adoration of the Magi,* a canvas stated by some to be by **Titian,** though others have doubted this. It is nevertheless superior to the replica in the Ambrosiana.

N.º 42, *Ecce Homo,* by **Titian** (?), work dubiously attributed.

N.º 289, *Agnese, sister-in-law of the painter,* by **Bernardino Liccinio** (1489-1549); **N.º 269,** *The Adoration of the Shepherds,* by **Palma «the Elder»** (1480-1528), a picture of good composition and colour quality, whose authenticity was originally questioned; **N.º 262,** *An officer,* portrait by **G. B. Moroni** (1520-1578).

ROOM XXVI.—RIBERA

José de Ribera (1591-1652), better known as **«El Españoleto»,** regarded as one of the greatest painters of the 17th century, was a pupil of **Ribalta.** In early youth he went to Napoles, where, under the protection of the Viceroy the Duke of Osuna, he lived most of his life and produced his works. **Ribera** is a good draughtsman and knows all the resources of colour, and should be studied in the very personal tecnique of chiaroscuro, of which he is best representative. No-one has equalled him in the painting of the seminude figure against a black and partially lit background. Very typical of **Ribera** are those grand scenes of martyrdoms, in sober tones of colour and filled with religious dramatism. But he is not only a painter in sombre hues, made up of contrasts of light and shade; his artistic career began here, and gradually evolved towards his richly coloured pictures of Virgins and female saints of remarkable beauty.

Among the pictures by him in this room, some belong to a set of Apostles.

N.º 1083, *St. James the Greater;* **N.º 1100,** *St. Bartholomew;* **N.º 1075,** *St. Paul the hermit;* **N.º 1118,** *Jacob receiving the benediction of Isaac;* **N.º 1106,** *St. Mary of Egypt;* **N.º 1105,** *The penitent Magdalene;* **N.º 1109,** *St. Roch.*

N.º 1069, *The Trinity,* This is one of **Ribera's** best and most important works; perfect, majestic in conception and full of gentle calm. A canvas dated about 1636, bought by Ferdinand VII for this Gallery. There is a similar one at the Escorial.

N.º 1108, *St. John the Baptist;* **N.º 1078,** *St. Andrew* (Plate 41).

N.º 1117, *The dream of Jacob,* a work of his last period, of good colouring and grandiose in conception, with a fine study of the Patriarch's head. This picture, originally attributed to **Murillo,** formed part of the collection of Isabel de Farnesio, whence it passed to the San Fernando Academy of Fine Arts, and finally to the Prado.

N.º 1072, *St. Peter, Apostle,* with the keys and a book.

N.º 1103, *The Magdalene* or *St. Thais,* a full-lenght female figure, kneeling, which belonged to the Marqués de los Llanos. In 1772 it was in the Royal Palace, whence it came to the Prado; a Saint of extraordinary beauty, several times repeated by the artist.

N.º 1101, *The Martyrdom of Bartholomew,* one of the most typical of his style. Tremendous as is the vision, it attracts without appalling us. In the middle, the contorted body of the Saint, in which we see a finely proportioned nude. The work is not sombre as far as colouring is concerned; this picture is dated 1638 by the artist;

it first belonged to the Royal Palace before being transferred to the Prado.

ROOM XXVI A

Zurbarán (1598-1664), who may be regarded as the major painter of the Sevilian school, is scantily represented here. For a better study of him we recommend a visit to the Monastery of Guadalupe or the Seville Provincial Museum.

More reposeful than **Ribera** and brighter in colouring, **Zurbarán** is the painter of friars and Spanish religious; his spiritual themes are ascetic scenes from convent life, and his clients were generally the religious Orders —Mercedarians, Carthusians and Hieronymites— whose habits he painted marvellously. He also did a large number of still-lifes, some most interesting. His compositions is very simple; like *Ribera* he was addicted to contrasts of light and shadows, and his temperament was deeply religious and well balanced. His work shows us the monastic life, expressed in a devout and moderate religious ideal.

N.º 2992, *The Immaculate Conception,* purchased by the Ministry of National Education in 1956.

N.º 2803, a *Still-life,* of his first period, property of D. Francisco Cambó, who bequeathed it to the Prado in 1946.

N.º 1239, *St. Casilda,* was the daughter of the Moorish King Almacrín, who rulled Toledo from 1038 to 1075. The charitable damsel was very compassionate towards the Christian prisoners, and a popular lenged relates that she was caught by her father one day taking food to them. He sternly asked what she was carrying, and she replied «Roses». And when she opened the fold of her garment the foodstuffs had in fact been turned into flowers.

A solitary standing figure, with hardly any indication to mark its religious character; against the dark background, the rich dress of a lady of the period adorning the graceful figure which advances delicately bearing the flowers and looking at the beholder, it seems more like a court portrait than the picture of a Saint. It came to the Prado from the Royal Collections. Notice especially the colouring and delicacy in the draperies of the Saint's garments.

N.º 2888, *Flower piece*, with carnations, madonna lilies and a rose.

N.º 2594, *St. Luke* before Christ crucified. A picture with remarkable intensity of expression, in which some believe that the figure of the saint is a self-portrait of **Zurbarán.**

N.º 1244, *Hercules, hunting the wild boar in Erymanthus,* one of the eight panels of the same series which were painted for the gallery of the Room of the Kingdoms in the Palace of Buen Retiro.

N.º 3010, *St. Anthony of Padua.*

N.º 1246, *Hercules and Anterus.*

N.º 1242, *Hercules overpowering Geryon.*

N.º 2442, *St. Didacus of Alcalá.*

N.º 1246, *Hercules diverts the river Alpheus.*

N.º 2472, *St. James de la Marca,* painted for the chapel of San Diego at Alcalá de Henares, whence it was taken to the Museum of the Trinidad, the Convent of San Francisco el Grande, and finally to the Prado.

N.º 1250, *Hercules, in the agony caused by the poisoned robe of the Centaur Nessus.*

N.º 1245, *Hercules, capturing the mad Cretan bull.*

N.º 1249, *Hercules, slaying the hidra of Lerna.*

N.º 1237, *Apparition of the Apostle St. Peter to St. Peter*

Nolasco. Both works were purchased by Ferdinand VII; they display the artist's extraordinary simplicity, together with a very good study of the natural highlights of the white in the Saint's robes.

N.º **656,** *Defence of Cadiz against the English*, by **Zurbarán.**

N.º **1236,** *Vision of St. Peter Nolasco* painted in 1629 for the cloister of the Mercedarian Convent at Seville, together with

N.º **1247,** *Hercules and the Cerberus.*

N.º **1243,** *Hercules, fighting the Nemean lion.*

ROOM XXVII

This room occupies the third section of the Central Gallery and is really the centre connecting the two wings of the Gallery.

In the middle, above, is a bust of the Prado architect, Juan de Villanueva; below, one of Charles V by **Pompeo Leoni,** and at the sides the equestrian portraits N.º **1176,** *Philip III*, and N.º **1177,** his wife *Queen Margarita of Austria*, are works from the studio of **Velázquez,** done by his pupils under his supervision. Facing these, N.º **1213,** *The Fountain of the Tritons*, landscape of the Island Garden at Aranjuez, believed to be by **Velázquez,** and N.º **1214,** *The Calle de la Reina at Aranjuez*, landscape by **Martínez del Mazo,** a pupil and son-in-law of **Velázquez.**

ROOM XXVIII.—MURILLO

Bartolomé Esteban Murillo (1618-1682) is the artist of delicacy and grace, lovable gentleness and popular religious feeling, far removed from the sternness of **Ribera** and the austerities of **Zurbarán. Murillo** is the

painter of the people's religion, and for it he painted
his figures, Virgins, children, and saints, filled with a
homely mysticism which informs all his works. Hence
his success in his day; but besides this he is a good painter,
delicate in colouring and perfect in draughtsmanship,
a simple, kindlay, man, of modest condition, who mostly
lived in Seville, without trips to Italy or approaches to
the Court.

His clients were the convents, particularly the Franciscan Order, for whom most of his work was done. In
general, he did not feel **Velázquez'** preoccupation with
the problem of light. His backgrounds have no other
object but to make figures stand out, for on the latter
he focussed his whole interest and attention.

N.º 962, *The Good Shepherd* (Plate XVI); **N.º 963,**
St. John the Baptist as a child; **N.º 964,** *The cildren of the
shell,* are three beautiful child studies, full of delicacy
and exquisite charm.

N.º 969, *The Descent of the Virgin to reward St. Ildefonso,* from the Isabel de Farnesio collection. From the
same collection come the three Immaculate Conceptions
(the painter's favoutite theme), in which we see the Virgin, depicted as almost a little girl, clad in white dress
and blue mantle, ascending to heaven amid golden cloud
effects and cherubs' heads.

N.º 972, *The Escorial Immaculate Conception;* **N.º 974,**
The Aranjuez Immaculate Conception, and **N.º 2809,** *The
Soult Immaculate Conception,* so called from the French
Marshal who carried it off from Seville to France in 1813.
There it stayed until an exchange of art works with the
French Government allowed it to be brought to the
Prado in 1941. This is the best of the three Immaculate
Conceptions here, and the most beautiful he ever painted.

N.º 978, *The appearance of the Virgin to St. Bernard,* both
from the Isabel de Farnesio collection.

N.º **995** and **994,** *The patrician's dream:* two large broader-than-long canvases, painted to adorn the church of Santa María la Blanca at Seville, in 1664.

N.º **2845,** *Gentleman in a ruff* (Plate 42), perhaps the last portrait painted by **Murillo.**

ROOM XXIX.—SPANISH SCHOOL OF THE 16TH AND 17TH CENTURIES
(Central Gallery)

A painter of the Madrid schools is **José Antolínez** (1635-1675), who may have been a pupil of **Francisco de Rizi. Antolínez** is a good colourist, who painted religious compositions, of which we notice the following here.

N.º **591,** *The Transitus of the Magdalene* (Plate 43), brought to the Prado in 1829.

One of his important works is the *Immaculate Conception*, at present on the Lower Floor, which we shall see later.

Next, three on religious themes suitable for altarpieces, by **Claudio Coello,** who was Court Painter to Charles II «the Bewitched», above all a good portraitist and a very complete artist because he was also a master of fresco and decoration. By him we have three canvases in which Flemish influences are to be seen, especially in the compositions, which are filled with subsidiary details that place them in the baroque class.

N.º **664,** *The triumph of St. Augustine*, dated 1664, from the Augustinians of the Strict Observance, at Alcalá de Henares.

N.º **660,** *The Virgin and Child* amid the theological virtues and saints.

N.º **661,** *The Virgin and Child worshipped by St. Louis,* *king of France*, a picture purchased by Charles III from the Marqués de la Ensenada.

Francisco de Herrera «the Younger» (1622-1685), son of **F. de Herrera «the Elder»,** also a painter. The younger **Herrera** went to Italy for six years and returned full of Baroque influences and brilliant details, which give his pictures an excessively flamboyant note, no doubt due to his own somewhat vain character. By him we have, **N.º 833,** *The triumph of St. Hermenegild* (Plate 44), for the high altar of the Madrid convent of Discalced Carmelites.

Juan Carreño de Miranda (1614-1685) was a pupil of **Velázquez.** Here we have his portrait **N.º 642,** *King Charles II* (Plate 45), and **N.º 644** *Queen Mariana of Austria* (Plate 46), the king's mother; **N.º 650,** *The Duke of Pastrana;* all three well conceived, very lifelike and correctly painted.

N.º 2806, *The miracle of the well,* bassed on an episode in the life of St. Isidro the Farm-Worker, done for the church of Santa María by the architect, sculptor and painter **Alonso Cano,** an artist of asto-nishing talent and a companion of Velázquez, who lived from 1601 to 1667.

P. Núñez de Villavicencio (1644-1700), a painter of the Andalusian school, following the footsteps of **Murillo,** whose art he is at great pains to emulate but seldom succeeds in doing.

N.º 1235, *Children playing:* this picture, showing children playing at dice, is much like of **Murillo** in theme, but we at once notice its inferiority, far below the charm of **Murillo's** *pilletes.* The canvas was later enlarged at the top to make it match another one and form a pair. The enlargement work is thought to be by the Italian **Lucca Giordano.**

Mateo Cerezo (1626-1666) is another of the Madrid

school. He is a complete artist and a good colourist who cultivates beauty and grace of form and is much given to religious themes. We now have two of his: **N.º 658,** *The Assumption of the Virgin to Heaven*, and **N.º 659,** *The mystical betrothal of St. Catherine of Alexandria*, purchased by Ferdinand VII; there is a replica in Palencia Cathedral.

Lastly, **N.º 980,** *St. Augustine between Christ and the Virgin by* **Murillo.**

ROOM XXX.—EL GRECO

See the description given after Rooms X and XI.

ROOM XXX A

This recently created room is wholly devoted to several XVII painters of the Spanish school.

N.º 1158, *Unknown personage*, by **Luis Tristán.**

N.º 3058, *Beheaded Saint*, by **Francisco Herrera el Viejo.**

N.º 3077, *St. Bede the Venerable*, by **Bartolomé Román.**

N.º 1034, *Unknown personage*, by **Pantoja.**

N.º 1065, *St. John and St. Matthew*, by **Ribalta.**

N.º 3004, *Portrait of his mother* (?), by **Antonio Puga.** The frontal figure, sitting down in a room so furnished as to evoke some Galician air.

N.º 1062, *St. Francis comforted by an angel*, by **Ribalta.** We see the painter's abilities in the quality of the colour, the half-light and the figure of the Saint, whom he has sought to depict not as beautiful, but as real; this

picture, purchased by Charles IV in 1801 from a Valencia
Capuchin community, was taken to the Palace at Aranjuez, and afterwards came to the Prado.

The Madrilenian **Fray Juan Rizi de Guevara** (1600-
1681), known as the Castilian **Zurbarán,** is the author
of **N.º 2510,** *St. Benedict blessing a loaf.*

N.º 2510, *St. Benedict, blessing the bread,* by **Rizi.**

N.º 2595, *Knight,* by **Maino.**

N.º 2802, *Still-life,* by **Felipe Ramírez.**

N.º 2441, *St. Bonaventure asks for the Franciscan habit,*
by **Francisco Herrera el Viejo.**

N.º 1037, *Queen Isabel de Borbon, first wife of Philip IV*
(Plate 39), a magnificent portrait in every way, by an
anonymous artist, which may be classified in the Madrid
school about 1620.

N.º 1164, *Still Life,* by **Van der Hamen.**

N.º 3080, *St. James the Less,* by **Antonio Arias.**

N.º 2600, *The supper of St. Benedict.*

N.º 3079, *The Apostle St. Thomas,* by **Antonio Arias.**

N.º 2836, *St. Mónica;* **N.º 2837,** *Weeping saint,* by
Luis Tristán (d. 1624).

N.º 593, *Flower-pot,* by **Arellano.**

N.º 1165, *Fruit-basket,* by **Van der Hamen.**

N.º 2833, *Brother Lucas Texero,* before the corpse of the
Venerable Father Bernardino of Obregón, dated 1627,
by a Spanish anonymous painter.

The Venerable lies dead; showing half of his figures,
Brother Texero is pointing to him and holds in his hand
his book «New Prayer and new Canticle to the Crown
of our Lady».

N.º 592, *Flower-pot,* by **Arellano.**

ROOM XXXI

This is really a passage running round the inner courtyard and the circular **Goya** Room, and is devoted to painters of the Italian, French and Spanish schools of the 17th and middle 18th centuries.

First, the portraits N.º **2329**, *Philip V*, and N.º **2330**, *Isabel de Farnesio* his wife, both by **J. Ranc,** a Frenchman (1674-1735).

Others of the same school are: several landscapes by **J. Vernet** (1714-1789); N.º **2289**, *St. John the Baptist*, by **Pierre Mignard** (1612-1693); N.º **2325**, *Flowerpiece*, by **F. Pret;** N.º **2242**, *Battle*, and N.º **2243**, *Skirmish*, by **J. Courtois,** known as **«Le Bourguignon»** (1621-1676), and N.º **2883**, *The Coliseum*, by **Hubert Robert** (1733-1808).

Vicente López Portaña (1772-1850) is a good pupil of **Maella,** whom we regard as a society painter, and who still has liveliness of colour and features, but overstresses details of dress and coiffure; in consequence, his portraits have the gaudiness of chromos. This is well shown by several royal portraits hanging here.

N.º **870 B,** *Queen María Cristina;* N.º **870,** *Colonel Juan Zengoitia Bengoa;* N.º **870 A,** *Ferdinand VII;* N.º **867,** *Queen María Josefa Amalia;* N.º **869,** *Doña María Isabel de Braganza;* N.º **2690,** *Fray Tomás Gascó;* N.º **2558,** *Señora de Carvallo;* N.º **868,** *Doña María Antonia de Borbón,* and N.º **866,** *The Infante Don Antonio.*

Luis Eugenio Menéndez or **Meléndez** (1716-1780), known as «the Spanish Chardin», is an artist who specialized in still-lifes, which he takes great pains with and paints marvellously, down to the tiniest details. Several hang on the walls of this room.

By **Antonio Carnicero** (1748-1814), a painter of the

end of the 18th century, we have the portrait **N.º 2649,** *Doña Tomasa Salcedo Aliaga,* and **N.º 641,** *Ascent of a balloon in Madrid,* a curious picture, in which the figures form a contemporary fashion-plate.

Domenico Tiepolo (1727-1804) was a Venetian, the son of the decorator Giovanni Battista. In 1772 he did three canvases for the church of San Felipe Neri. **N.º 358,** *Christ on the road to Calvary;* **N.º 359,** *El Expolio* (Christ stripped of His garments), and **N.º 632,** *The burial of Christ;* the rest of this series can be seen on the Upper Floor of the Gallery.

By **Corrado Giaquinto** (1700-1765), an Italian who was a decorator rather than an artist, there are the following: **N.º 108,** *Descending from the Cross;* **N.º 105,** *The sacrifice of Iphigeneia;* **N.º 106,** *The battle of Clavijo;* **N.º 107,** *The Prayer in the Garden,* and **N.º 103,** *Birth of the Sun.*

These are followed by several works of another Italian, **G. Panini** (1692-1765).

The Valencian-born **Mariano Salvador Maella** (1739-1819) is here represented by five paintings, simple and sugary, very much in the style of the period and influenced by his master **Rafael Mengs;** four of them depict the Seasons **N.ºˢ 2497-2500** and the other is a *Seascape,* **N.º 873.**

Another Valencian, **Agustín Esteve** (1753-1820) has two portraits: **N.º 2581,** *Doña Joaquina Téllez Girón,* daughter of the Duke of Osuna, and **N.º 2876,** *Don Mariano San Juan y Pinedo,* a child portrait, well done and very handsome. There are also several works by second-class painters.

ROOM XXXII.—GOYA

The works by Goya, totalling 103 pictures in addition to the 485 drawings, have been hung by groups in ten rooms, namely nine in succession on the Lower Floor of the building, and this room on the Main Floor, which fits in well with a visit to the Central Gallery, devoted to Spanish painters.

The painter **Francisco de Goya** (1746-1828) is a very remarkable case in 18th-century Spanish painting. Art which had reached such a high level in earlier periods, was now sunk in veritable prostration, owing to preciosity and the exaggerated imitation of a false academicism with formulae repeated to excess. Amid this, when all seemed lost, appeared the figure of the Aragonese painter **Goya,** with his extraordinary personality, and raised Spanish painting again to a great height.

He had boundless vigour and his work is monumental; he tackled everything, in the most widely diverse genres, and his pictures forcibly display the character and talent with which they were conceived: politicians, royalties, writers, bullfighters, clerics and aristocrats; his work ranges from portraits to tapestry cartoons, and he used the most widely diverse media: oil, drawing, etching, lithography, fresco, tempera.

He was a contemporary of **Antón-Rafael Mengs,** who at first gave him work, and of **Francisco Bayeu,** whose sister he later married. His extraordinary qualities were not long in appearing.

We know that like **Velázquez** he went to Italy where we find him struggling for recognition in his early days. The vast work of **Goya,** to be understood properly, calls for a detailed classification of his pictures.

In the first place, we have the **Goya** of the portraits;

next, as a historical painter; thereafter, as author of manners-and-modes pieces or scenes for tapestries; and lastly, as creator of the visions of his last period («black paintings»), and in his drawings.

In this Room we see one of his best works in the portrait genre: **N.º 726,** *The family of Charles IV*, painted at Aranjuez in 1800, whence it went to the Madrid Royal Palace and then to the Prado. We here see details of the technique that **Velázquez** used in the *Meninas*, but without attaining the same perfection. The group painting has somewhat the air of a family photograph, with the royal pair in the foreground, and then the princes, princesses and grandchildren, to the number of thirteen persons in all. To the beholder's left, and in the middle distance, is the painter, facing a canvas of which only a part is visible. The picture is correct in drawing, though the most important thing is the extraordinary quality of the colour in fresh, brilliant tones which give it life; it looks more like a real scene than a picture, in which we observe the perfect drawing of the types, whose faces reflect the faults and virtues of their lives, the former rather than the latter. Despite the excesive number of figures, all are well portrayed, in some cases with too much expressivenes and perhaps with rather pointed irony.

On the right and left of the Room, the equestrian portraits of **N.º 720,** *Queen María Luisa* and **N.º 719,** *King Charles IV*, a matching pair, painted for the Madrid Royal Palace in 1799.

Next come the studies from the life which were used to compose picture **N.º 726,** namely: **N.º 729,** *Princess María Josefa;* **N.º 730,** *Don Francisco de Paula;* **N.º 731,** *Don Carlos María Isidro* (Plate 47); **N.º 732,** *Don Luis de Borbón*, Prince of Parma, and **N.º 733,** *The Infante Don Antonio Pascual.*

El Buen Pastor.—The Good Shepherd.—Le Bon Pasteur.—Der göttliche
Hirte.—Il Buon Pastore

**La Reina Artemisa.—Queen Artemis.—La Reine Artémise.—Die Königin
Artemisia.—La Regina Artemisa**

La degollación del Bautista.—The Beheading of Saint John Baptist.—La Décapitation de St.-Jean-Baptiste.—Die Enthauptung Johannes der Taufer.—La Decapitazione di S. Giovanni Battista

San Pedro Mártir en oración.—The Martyr Saint Peter at Prayer.
St.-Pierre Martyr en prière.—Der heilige Petrus Martyr im Gebet.
S. Pietro Martire in preghiera

Cristo bendiciendo.—Christ blessing.—Jésus-Christ donnant sa Bénédiction.—Christus segnend.—Gesù Cristo mentre benedice

La Virgen de los Reyes Católicos.—The Virgin of the Catholic Sovereigns.
La Vierge des Rois Catholiques.—Die Jungfrau der Katholischen Könige.
La Madonna dei Re Cattolici

La Adoración de los Magos.—The Adoration of the Magi.—L'Adoration des Mages.—Die Anbetung der Könige.—L'Adorazione dei Re Magi

La Reina Isabel de Borbón, mujer de Felipe IV.—The Queen Isabella de Bourbon.—La Reine Isabelle de Bourbon.—Die Königin Elisabeth von Bourbon.—La Regina Isabella di Borbone, sposa di Filippo IV

San Jerónimo.—Saint Jerome.—St.-Jérôme.—Der heilige Hyeronymus.
S. Gerolamo

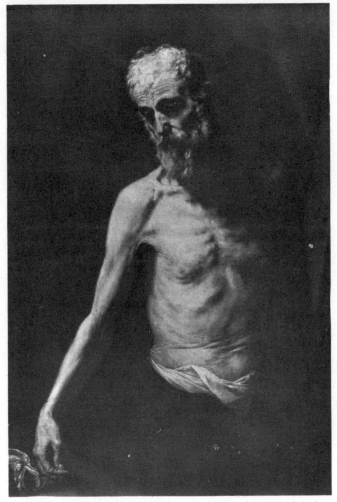

San Andrés.—Saint Andrew.—St. André.—Der Heilige Andreas.—S. Andrea

**Caballero de Golilla.—Gentleman's portrait.—Le chevalier de rabat.
Bildnis eines Edelmannes.—Il Cavaliere di Golilla**

**Tránsito de la Magdalena.—The Assumption of Mary Magdalen.—Pas-
sage de la Madeleine.—Maria Magdalenas Himmelsfahrt.—La salita
in Cielo di Maria Maddalena**

**Apoteosis de San Hermenegildo.—The Triumph of St. Hermenegild.
Le triompho de St.-Herménégilde.—Triumph des heiligen Hermenegil-
dus.—Apoteosi di S. Ermenegildo**

Retrato de Carlos II.—Charles II's portrait.—Charles II.—Karl II.
Ritratto di Carlo II

Retrato de Doña Mariana de Austria.—Portrait of the Queen Mariana of Austria.—La Reine Marianne d'Autriche.—Die Königin Marianne von Österreich.—Ritratto di Marianna d'Austria

Lám. 46

Retrato del Infante D. Carlos María Isidro.—Portrait of the Infant D. Carlos María Isidro.—L'Infant D. Carlos María Isidro.—Bild des Infanten D. Carlos María Isidro.—Ritratto dell'Infante Carlo María Isidro

Doña Tadea Arias de Enríquez

GOYA (1746-1828)

La maja vestida

General Ricardos

La Maja desnuda.—The «Maja» naked.—La «Maja» nue.—Die umbekleidete «Maja».—La «Maja Desnuda»

Louis XVI

La Infanta Doña Ana Victoria de Borbón

El Parnaso.—The Parnassus.—Le Parnasse.—Der Parnass.—Il Parnaso

La Purísima Concepción.—Immaculate Conception.—L'Immaculée Conception.—Die unbefleckte Empfägnis.—L'Immacolata Concezione

Carlos III comiendo ante su corte.—Charles III at Meal.—Charles III déjeunant devant sa cour.—Karl III speist in Genenwart seines Hofes.—Carlo III mentre sta mangiando dinanzi alla Corte

Retrato del pintor Goya.—A portrait of Goya.—Portrait du peintre Goya.
Bildnis Goyas.—Ritratto del pittore Goya

Los desposorios de la Virgen.—The Marriage of the Virgin.—Le Marriage de la Vierge.
Die Vermahlüng der heiligen Jungfrau.—Lo Sposalizio della Madonna

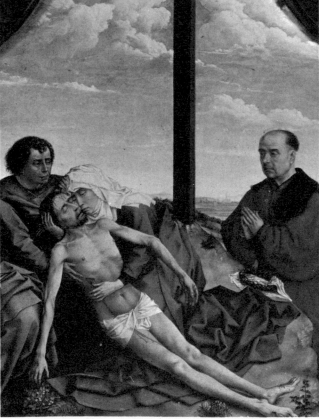

La Piedad.—Pieta.—La Piété.—Das Mitleid.—La Pietà

El Descendimiento de la Cruz (detalle).—The Descending of the Cross.
La Descente de Croix.—Die Kreuzabnahme.—La Deposizione dalla Croce.

**La Natividad.—The Nativity.—La Nativité.—Die Geburt Jesu.—La Nas-
cita di Gesù**

Descanso en la huida a Egipto.—The Rest on the Flight into Egypt.—Repos dans la fuite en Egypte.—Ruhe auf der Flucht nach Aegypte.—Sosta durante la Fuga in Egitto

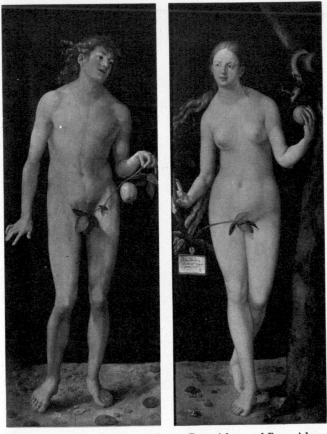

**Adán y Eva.—Adam and Eve.—Adam et Eve.—Adam und Eva.—Adamo
et Eva**

El Jardín de las Delicias (detalle).—The Garden of the Delights.—Le Jardin des Délices.—Der Garten der Vergnügen.—Il Giardino delle Delizie

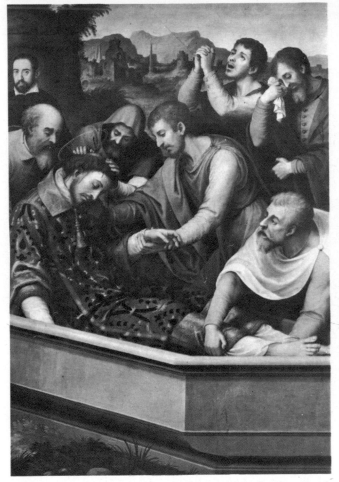

Entierro de San Esteban.—Saint Stephen's burial.—Enterrement de
St.-Etienne.—Beerdigung des heiligen Stephans.—La sepultura di
S. Stefano (?)

General Urrutia.—Bildnis des Generals Urrutia.—Il Generale Urrutia

Next, the delicate portrait **N.º 734,** *Isidoro Máiquez*, the great actor, and **N.º 722,** *Josefa Bayeu de Goya?*, his wife.

N.º 2448, *The Marquesa de Villafranca*, Doña Tomasa Palafox, daughter of the Countess of Montijo.

N.º 740, *Doña Tadea Arias de Enríquez* (Plate 48), a fine portrait with marvellous grey shadings.

The superb portrait **N.º 2784,** *General Ricardos* (Plate 49).

N.º 721, his brother-in-law *Francisco Bayeu*, painted in 1795, shortly before his death. This is a marvellous portrait, undoubtedly the best he ever did; unerring in the grey colouring, in which he actually dispensed with vermilion; even the priming òf the canvas is done with a reddish grey; the figure, in which the eyes are outstanding, is without blemish and in full light. The accuracy of the brushwork is amazing.

On either side of the doorway, we see the two Majas: **N.º 741,** *The Maja clothed* (Plate XVII), and **N.º 742,** *The Maja nude* (Plate 50). These two pictures are very celebrated, and there are a number of stories and legends, largely created by popular fancy, concerning the identity of the model. Both must be dated 1797 or 1798, and were for a long time in Godoy's collection, where they were known as *Gitanas* (gypsies). After this, they were in the San Fernando Academy for a while, before being finally placed in the Prado in 1901.

The model, setting aside the legends that made her the Duchess of Alba, is more like a true popular type representing the ideal beauty of the period. It is true that the features and face show a striking resemblance to the Duchess of Alba; but a detailed examination of the canvas of the *Maja nude*, carried out by the present Director of the Prado Gallery, Sr. Sotomayor, has proved that the head does not fit well on the neck, which suggests that the body was painted first and the head added afterwards. The two pictures show a different technique: the nude figure is carefully done in minute brushwork, and the clothed one in haste with heavy strokes. The nude is a small figure, with the body delicate, well-proportioned and perfectly modelled. In both, grey shading predominantes, with little mass of warm colouring. These are the two most popular pictures of the Aragonese genius, *The Maja clothed* and *The Maja nude*, and «we cannot tell if she is more clothed when nude, or more nude when clothed».

Lastly we have the portrait **N.º 736,** *General Urrutia* (Plate XVIII); the Cross of St. George that he wears was conferred on him by Catherine of Russia in 1789. A magnificently lifelike portrait.

In the upper part of the room, **N.ᵒˢ 2546** and **2548,** two out of three canvases from the Palace of Godoy allegorically representing Agriculture and Commerce.

ROOM XXXIII.—FRENCH PAINTING

This minute room, which serves as an anteroom to Room XXXIV, contains a large portrait, **N.º 2238,** in a sumptuous gilt frame, of *Louis XVI* (Plate 51), by **A. F. Callet,** a Frenchman. It was presented by the King himself to the Spanish Ambassador Count Aranda, in 1783.

ROOM XXXIV.—FRENCH PAINTING (Continued.)

French painting, less realistic than Spanish, seeks its inspiration in a learned classicism, emanating from Rome and Bologna, and is excessively preocupied with theme and emotion. **Poussin, Watteau, Mignard, Van Loo** and **Claude «de Lorrain»,** and others, display balanced compositions, full of classical notes, perhaps frívolous at times, but without losing their aristocratic air; all this within the bounds of good taste, and with frequently marvellous drawing and colouring.

Louis-Michel van Loo (1707-1771), an artist who lived for some years in Spain, is the author of the eye-filling **N.º 2283,** entitled *The family of Philip V*. This vast canvas well displays the features of the Bourbon period: sumptuosity, luxury, excessive pomp, and mannerism. There stand all the personages composing the Royal Family, in meaningless, artificial attitudes; all very rich but frigid.

Jean Ranc (1674-1735), another painter whom Philip V patronized, lived for several years in Spain, and died there. He is represented by a number of royal portraits.

N.º 2333, *Ferdinand VI*, as a child; **N.º 2334,** *Charles III*, as a child; **N.º 2335,** *Ferdinand VI when Prince of Asturias* (Crown Prince); **N.º 2332,** *Luisa Isabel de Orléans*, Queen of Spain, and **N.º 2376,** *The family of Philip V*.

Nicholas Largillière (1656-1746) was a good painter of portraits and was known as «the French Van Dyck», **N.º 2277**, is a delicate and well-executed portrait of the Infanta *María Ana Victoria de Borbón* (Plate 52).

Michel Angel Houasse (1680-1730) was Philip V's first court painter. **N.º 2387** is his fine portrait of *Luis I* as a child, perfectly executed, in grey tones reminiscent of the Velázquez manner, and **N.º 2269,** *View of the Monastery of El Escorial*.

N.º 2358, portrait of *Doña María Amelia of Saxony*, by **Luis Silvestre,** and **N.º 2350,** *Seascape*, a small picture by **Vernet.**

ROOM XXXV.—FRENCH PAINTING (Continued.)

Nicholas Poussin (1594-1665), a Norman, regarded as the best painter of his day, and the most philosophical of French artists, was a keen student of classical art, from which he drew his themes and characters. His work always shows firm modelling, and he arranged his compositions around a presiding idea. He copies his grandiose themes from the Roman countryside, and on this basis he reconstructs Nature as if it were architecture in reverse. An academic painter, much influenced by **Raphael,** he was endowed with a great portical sense, which sometimes has an effect even on his colour.

One of this artist's best works is **N.º 2320,** *Meleager's hunt*, or *The Triumph of Aeneas*, in which his talent for drawing and colouring can be noted, together with the movement and sense of life that the figures give; **N.º 2308,** *Landscape with ruins of ancient Rome;* **N.º 2307,** *Landscape;* **N.º 2310,** *Broken country with foliage*, and **N.º 2322,** *Polyphemus and Galatea*.

N.º 2319, *Landscape with Diana asleep*, is by a pupil of **Poussin.**

Pierre Mignard (1612-1693) is a good pupil of **Vouet,** regarded as one of the best French portraitists; he is represented by **N.º 2291,** *The Infanta María Teresa de Austria*.

N.ºs 2353, *Marriage capitulations and Country dance*, and **2354,** *Party in a park* are two pretty pictures, the only ones in the Gallery by **Watteau** (1684-1721), a painter with a subtle technique whose works always preserve their pictorial sense with small impressionist touches. **Watteau** is the most faithful interpreter of *fêtes galantes*, society pleasures and bucolic idylls. His painting is free, nervous and most attractive in colouring, with a certain poetical spirituality which is reflected in his scenes of picnics, open-air concerts and conversations in parks.

In addition, there are several royal portraits: **N.º 2343,** *Louis XIV*, and **N.º 2337,** *Philip V*, both by **Rigaud** (1659-1743), and others of lesser importance.

ROOM XXXVI.—FRENCH PAINTING (Continued.)

N.º 2259, *The penitent Magdalene*, by **Claude «Le Lorrain»** (1600-1682), a painter of spiritual lanscapes steeped in classicism.

N.º 2318, *Bacchic scene;* **N.º 2313,** *Parnassus* (Plate 53); **N.º 2311,** *The triumph of David*, and **N.º 2317,** *St. Cecily*, all five by **N. Poussin;** these pictures display his talent and qualities and are conceived with a poetical sense, even in colour.

The types are conventional, with a certain air of statuary, but they are excellent in colouring, whic is the best feature of the picture. *The Bacchanal* is dated 1636 and was one of the pictures belonging to Philip V at La Granja; the scene is highly rationalized and full of successes in the arrangement and modelling of the figures, though one observes a lack of vigour and we miss the vitality of **Titian's** bacchanals.

Claude «Le Lorrain» (1600-1682) is the author of **N.ºs 2254,** *St. Paula of Rome embarking at Ostia;* **2255,** *The Archangel Raphael and Tobias;* **2253,** *Landscape: Moses saved from the waters;* **2252,** *Landscape: Burial of St. Serapia.*

Unnumbered *Pleasures and Time*, by **Simon Vouet** (1590-1649), and **N.º 2240,** *Louis XIII* of France, by **Champaigne** (1602-1674).

These rooms also contain three equestrian statues, of Louis XIV, Philip V, and an unknown prince. Their sculptor is anonymous.

ROOM XXXVII.—ITALIAN PAINTERS OF THE 16TH AND 17TH CENTURIES

N.º **86,** *Jacob's journey;* N.º **88,** *Diogenes looking for a man;* N.º **87,** *Concert,* and N.º **94,** *Expulsion of the money-changers from the Temple,* by **Benedetto Castiglioni,** painter and engraver (1616-1670).

N.º **144,** *Lot and his daughters,* a rather unequal painting by the Florentine **Francesco Furine** (1600-1646).

N.º **65,** *David defeats Goliath,* attributed to **Michelangelo Americhi «il Caravaggio»** (1560-65 to 1609), and N.º **246,** *St. Margaret raises a lad from the dead,* by **Giovanni Serodine.**

N.º **327,** *The painter Andrea Sacchi,* portrait by **Carlo Maratti** (1625-1713).

N.º **326,** portrait of *Francesco Albani,* by **Andrea Sacchi.**

N.º **201,** *Susanna and the Elders,* from the Monastery of El Escorial, by **Francesco Barbieri, «il Guercino»** (1591-1665), a painter of the Italian school.

Lastly, N.º **145,** *Interior of the Basilica of St. Peter at Rome,* by the architect and painter **Filippo Gagliardi,** and N.º **210,** *The Madonna of the Chair,* by **Guido Reni.**

ROOM XXXVIII.—ITALIAN PAINTING
(Continued.)

This room contains a series of works by Italian painters, all falling within the current canons and the too-often repeated formulae of the great masters, so that the painters' personalities are frequently swamped. They are impeccable canvases, without a single touch of originality.

The most important figure in this group is **Guido Reni,** of Bologna (1575-1642), who has been accused of forging Caravaggios. He was a cultivated artist, and a man of gallantry and elegance to whose lot it fell to live in a stormy period of quarrels and treacheries; he knew his craft well, and we have some of his works on religious themes, handsome and well painted, but over-smooth and affected. By him are **N.º 211,** *St. Sebastian,* a theme he repeated several times; **N.º 208,** *Lucretia taking her own life,* and **N.º 216,** *The penitent Magdalene.*

Next, **N.º 2475,** *A cleric,* by **P. M. Neri** (?) (1601-1661).

N.º 128, *Pietà,* and **N.º 129,** *The Scourging,* both by **Danielle Crespi** (1590-1630), following in the footsteps of the foregoing, with a good nude study of the figure of Christ; a copy hangs in the convent of the Augustinas at Salamanca.

N.º 877, *Self-portrait* by **O. Borgiani** (1578-1616).

N.º 353, *St. Cecily playing the organ,* by **L. Spada** (1576-1622).

N.º 131, *Abraham's sacrifice,* by **Domenico Zampieri, «il Domenichino»** (1581-1641).

N.º 2, *The Judgement of Paris;* **N.º 1,** *The toilet of Venus,* mythological themes, by **Francesco Albani,** of Bologna (1576-1600); lastly, **N.º 245,** *College Room in Venice,* by **Pietro Malombra** (1536-1618), and **N.º 91,** *Elephants in a circus,* by **Castiglione.**

ROOM XXXIX.—WORKS BY TIEPOLO, BATTONI, PARET, VICENTE LOPEZ AND OTHERS

Giovanni Battista Tiepolo (1696-1770), a Venetian who still maintained the colourist tradition of his birthplace, came to Spain at the invitation of Charles III to decorate the Madrid Royal Palace, and this forms the most important part of his work. A painter of powerful tecnique, spirited colouring and lively composition, he lived his last years in Spain. There are some of his pictures in this Room, but they lose by comparison with his frescos in the Royal Palace: **N.º 363,** *The Immaculate Conception* (Plate 54), painted for the church of San Pascual at Aranjuez in 1769; **N.º 365 A,** *St. Francis of Assisi receiving the Stigmata,* for the same church; **N.º 364,** *An Angel bearing the Eucharist,* which must have gone on the upper part of the high-altar reredos in the same church of San Pascual at Aranjuez. **N.º 364 A,** *St. Paschal Baylon;* **N.º 2691,** *Deliverance of the Apostle St. Peter.*

In these works we see notes of clearness and luminosity, with rich colouring full of reminiscences of Venetian painting.

N.º 2464, *Abraham and the three Angels,* based on a passage from *Genesis,* chapter XVIII, and painted for a ceiling, and **N.º 365,** *Olympus,* a sketch of unknown origin showing Jupiter, Juno, Diana, Minerva, Venus, Mercury and Saturn; **N.º 2900,** *St. Paschal Baylon,* and **N.º 583,** *Angel with crown of lilies.*

Luis Paret y Alcázar (1746-1799), a Madrid painter who specialized in the painting of flowers, an artist of refined, delicate technique, offers us his little cabinet pictures, delicately executed and filled with graceful little figures, worthy of comparison with those of **Watteau. N.º 2422,** *Charles III dining in the presence of his court* (Plate 55), signed jokingly by the artist in Greek characters. This was in the Palace of Gatchina in Russia, and came to the Prado in 1933; the beautiful little picture. **N.º 2875,** *Masked Ball,* was acquired by the Prado Trust in 1944. We shall see more of this painter's work on the Upper Floor.

Cristo presentado al pueblo.—Christ shown to the people.—Le Christ presenté au peuple.—Christus dem volk gezeigt.—Cristo presentato al popolo

El carro de heno (detalle).—The Hay Wain.—La charrette de foin.—Der Heuwagen.—Il Carro di fieno

The ceiling of the Room has a composition in tempera of the allegory of the *Donation of the Casino to Isabella of Braganza*, painted for the drawingroom of the mansion that the Council presented to Ferdinand VII's third wife in 1818. Can be more confortably viewed in the mirror on the back wall.

Next, several more portraits by **Vicente López Portaña,** a painter we have already mentioned, who received the greatest attentions from the King and Queen. Chiefly outstanding is the best portrait he ever painted, **N.º 864,** *The painter Francisco de Goya* (Plate 56); **N.º 2901,** *Don Antonio Ugarte and his wife;* and **N.º 865,** *Portrait of Doña María Cristina de Borbón*, a rather artificial figure, with excessive subsidiary details of clothing and coiffure.

There is also **N.º 49,** *A gentleman at Rome*, by **Pompeo Battoni**, an Italian (1708-1787), and **N.º 2882,** *Cardinal Carlo de Borgia*, by another Italian, **A. Procaccini** (1671-1734).

Finally, **N.º 109,** *St. Lawrence in Heaven*, by **Corrado Giaquinto** (1700-1765).

It we leave the entrance rotunda by the door on the right, we find ourselves in the section devoted to Flemish Primitives, namely a series of five rooms containing over 75 such works, all on wood.

ROOM XL.—FLEMISH PRIMITIVES

The County of Flanders and Duchy of Burgundy, with Bruges, Tournai and Brussels, politically united since the end of the 15th century, formed the place of origin of this universal school, whose influence was to have a powerful effect on all European painting. The basic features of the school are a tendency towards realism with exaggerated minuteness of detail.

We enter, turn right, and go the end where we can admire several panels and triptychs in oil, of magnificent quality and in a good state preservation. What is really surprising is the brilliance and purity of colouring, unfaded despite five centuries, of this chromatic symphony of intense blues, greens, golds and reds. The quality of the drawing is insuperable and exact down to the tiniest detail; nothing escapes the minute observation of an artist of this school, who is a conscientious master of his craft. The slightest detail of architecture, the smallest crease in the fold of a drapery, everything is completely captured by the retina of these great masters, with an attention to detail which may at times appear excessive, but never at the expense of composition. From Flanders their art spread all over Europe, and countless imitators arose, who seldon reached the same perfection. It is well known that Isabella the Catholic liked this remarkable painting, and formed an important collection of Flemish primitives.

First **N.º 2801,** *Christ presented to the people* (Plate XIX), the most important work of **Quintin Metsys** (1466-1530), of delicate quality and in a splendid state of preservation.

N.º 1461, *Triptych*, by **D. Bouts** (about 1420-1475). It shows four religious scenes: *The Annunciation, the Visitation, the Adoration of the Angels,* and *the Adoration of the Magis,* originally attributed to **Petrus Christus** but now classified as a first-period work of **Tierry Bouts** (1420?-1475).

N.ᵒˢ 1890 and **1892,** *The coin of Caesar*, two leaves from the triptych *The Redemption,* by **Van der Weyden** (1400-1464).

N.º 1559, triptych of the *Ecce-Homo*, attributed to the **Maestro de la Santa Sangre.**

N.º 1510, *Christ between the Virgin Mary and St. John the Baptist.* Copy of the figures on the altar of St. Bavo

(Ghent), made on paper stuck to a panel, by **Jan Gossart,** known as **Juan de Mabuse** (1478-1536).

N.º **1915,** *The Annunciation,* by the **Maestro de Flémalle;** also by him, **N.º 1887,** *Betrothal of the Virgin* (Plate 57), a magnificently coloured and perfectly drawn panel, in which the beauty of the Virgin's face is most noteworthy; also **N.ᵒˢ 1514,** *St. Barbara,* and **1513,** *St. John the Baptist.*

N.º **1617,** *St. Francis of Assisi receiving the Stigmata,* by the **Maestro de Hoogstraten.**

N.º **1511,** *The Fountain of Grace,* or *Triumph of the Church over the Synagogue,* attributed to the brothers **Van Eyck** or their school; it comes from the Monastery of Santa María del Parral (Segovia), and is based on a vision of, or legend about, the German 13th-century nun St. Hildegard. This panel is one of the best and most representative works of the Flemish school, through the arrangement of the figures, the colouring, and the fineness of the architectural details.

N.º **1921,** *The Virgin with the Child,* by **Petrus Christus** (d. 1473?).

N.º **2544,** *The Virgin, the Child, little St. John an three angels,* by **Isenbrandt** (1510-1551).

N.º **2538,** *Passages from the life of Christ,* triptych by an **anonymous Hispano-Flemish** painter.

N.º **2696,** *The Virgin with the Child* by a pupil of **Jan van Eyck.**

ROOM XLI.—FLEMISH PRIMITIVES (Continued.)

This small room contains two of the most eminet painters of the period, namely **Van der Weyden** and **Memling.** First, we have **N.º 2540,** *Pietà* (Plate 58), a panel of small size filled with emotion and piety, which captivates, above all, by the luminosity of its colours, so delicate and brillant that it appears quite modern. From the middle of the 19th century it belonged to the Duke of Mandas, and came into the Prado in 1925.

N.º **2825,** *The Descending of the Cross* (Plate 59): the dead Christ, the three Maries and the Holy Men; ten full-lenght figures upon a background of gold, standing out like sculptures of a reredos with a Gothic setting, also a very highly prized work, by **Van der Weyden,** painted about 1435 for a Louvain chapel; it was later acquired by Maria of Hungary, sister of Charles V, and sent to the Monastery of El Escorial. As is well known, Philip II was delighted with this work, and commissioned **Michel Coxcie** to make a copy, which is the picture that was in the Prado until it was exchanged for the original and the copy went to El Escorial. This is undoubtedly the author's masterpiece; it is a fundamental work of Flemish painting, with a surprising pathetism in the attitudes and faces of its figures, who form a dramatic scene, intense but natural, without artificialities or affected postures. Very interesting is the detail of extending the panel in the middle of the upper part, where we see the Cross prolonged, and the clever placing of the head of Joseph of Arimathaea, who is Lifting down from the Cross the dead body of Our Lord.

N.º **1920,** *The Virgin of the Milk*, by **Van Orley** (1492-1542).

N.º **2541,** *The Visitation of the Virgin to St. Elizabeth*, by **Juan de Flandes** (d. 1519).

N.º **2542,** *The Crucifixion*, a work by the school of **Gerard David.**

N.ᵒˢ **1888-1889-1891,** *The Redemption*, a triptych by **Van der Weyden** (1399?-1464), which at first was doubtfully attributed to him. It comes from the Convento de los Angeles in Madrid, and was acquired by the Prado in 1938. It represents the Crucifixion, the Virgin and St. John, against the background of a Gothic church; on either side, the *Expulsion from Eden* and the *Last Judgement;* below, the *Resurrection of the Body* and the *Separation of the Just from the Reprobates;* a well-executed painting of great expressiveness, with some interesting portions, especially the centre panel.

By **Hans Memling** (1433 - 1494) is a triptych —**N.º 1557**— with several scenes from the life of Christ: the *Nativity* (Plate 60), the *Epiphany* and the *Presentation in the Temple.* This work belonged to Charles V, and came to the Prado in 1847 from a castle near Aranjuez. It is very like another by the same painter in the Bruges Hospital, though apparently earlier; a most perfect panel, with amazing colouring and drawing, the whole of insuperable precision and quality.

By the same, **N.º 2543,** *The Virgin and Child between two angels,* a panel that has been bably restored.

N.º 1886, *The Crucifixion,* by a pupil of **Van der Weyden.**

N.º 2700, *St. Anne, the Virgin and the Child,* by **Jan de Cock,** a painter of the beginning of the 16th century.

N.º 1558, *The Adoration of the Magi,* by **Memling,** copy by **Van der Weyden,** and **N.º 2663,** the same theme by a pupil of **Van der Weyden.**

ROOM XLII.—FLEMISH PRIMITIVES (Continued.)

First, we have **N.º 1943,** *The Mass of St. Gregory,* by **Adriaen Isenbrandt** (d. 1551).

N.º 1609, *St. James the Greater and eleven praying figures;* **N.º 1610,** *St. John the Evangelist, two ladies and two girls in prayer,* and the triptych **N.º 2223,** *The Adoration of the Magi,* by **P. Coecke van Aelst** (1502-1550).

N.º **2692,** *The Holy Family*, and **N.º 1932,** *The Virgin with the Child*, both **Van Orley** (1492-1542); the later panel is very beautiful and is in the purest Flemish style of painting, with a very notable landscape background.

By **Jan Gossart de Maubege,** known as **Mabuse** (1478-1536?), there are two pictures here:

N.º **1930,** *The Virgin with the Child*, and **N.º 1536,** *The Virgin of Louvain;* this panel is doubtfully attributed; on the back there is a dedication by the author to Philip II for the favours for which the city of Louvain was indebted to him. The panel is nearer to the style of **Van** than **Gossart.**

N.º **2494,** triptych with *The Annunciation, St. Jerome* and *St. John the Baptist*, by the **Maestro de la Santa Sangre.**

N.º **1361,** triptych of *The Adoration of the Magi*, **anonymous Flemish,** and **N.ºˢ 1941** and **1942,** *St. Catherine* and *St. Barbara*, leaves of a triptych painted by the **Maestro de Francfort** (1460-1515?)

Gerard David (d. 1523), one of the greatest of Flemish painters, who closes the cycle begun by **Van Eyck,** and whose feeling of piety formed the whole content of his art, is the author of the following works: **N.º 1537,** *The Virgin with the Child;* **N.º 2643,** *Rest on the flight into Egypt* (Plate 61), a picture from the Bosch Bequest and one of the best in the Room, and **N.º 1512,** *The Virgin with the Child and two angels crowning her.*

ROOM XLIII.—FLEMISH PRIMITIVES
(Continued.)

Joaquin Patinir (1480-1524), the best of the Flemish landscapists, accentuates this aspect so much that at times the background swamps the theme itself. Here hangs one of his masterpieces, **N.º 1616,** *Passage of the Stygian lake:* Charon's boat is conveying a soul to Hades which is guarded by Cerberus. On the left, the Elysian Fields.

N.º 1615, *The temptations of St. Anthony,* in collaboration with **Massys. N.º 1614,** *Landscape with St. Jerome.* **N.º 1611,** *Rest during the flight into Egypt.* Attributed to his son **Henri Patinir** is **N.º 1612,** *Rest during the flight into Egypt,* which is also the title of **N.º 1613,** attributed to a pupil of **Patinir.**

N.º 2048, triptych of The Adoration of the Magis, by **Hieronymus van Aecken Bosh,** known in Spain as «**el Bosco**» (1450-1516); technically, his masterpiece. What define the character and artistic personality of **Bosch** are the audacious devilries which fill his paintings with tiny figures rioting crazily amid queer and unknown animals and vegetables.

In **N.º 2052,** *The hay wain* (Plate XX), in other words the waggon of fleshly delights, we see the wain pursued by the Pope, Emperor, King and other rulers, all trying to climb onto it, forgetting the biblical saying that all flesh is grass.

N.º 2056, *Extraction of the stone of madness;* **N.º 2049,** *The temptations of St. Anthony;* **N.º 2695,** *A crossbowman.* In some of his pictures, this artist of overflowing and fantastic imagination conveys to us an impression of his dreams, which are always variations on the problem of sin.

In the middle of the room stands **N.º 1622,** *The Table of the Mortal Sins,* also by **Bosch.** It comes from the Monastery of El Escorial, where it was highly esteemed by Philip II, who had it placed in his chamber. It is covered with a sheet of galss, and depicts Christ, the Man of Sorrows, surrounded by a border showing the seven deadly sins, and in the corners four circles with the Four Last Things: Death, Judgement, Hell and Heaven.

N.º **1393,** *The Triumph of Deat,* by **Brueghel «the Elder»** (1525-1569), a highly personal and surprising theme, perhaps the outcome of a macabre nightmare, a feverish moment contrasting with the character of the painter, who was much addicted to feasting and pleasure. A picture dated 1560, of good colouring, perfectly combined. It shows scenes on the road to the kingdom of death; against a background of mountains, with fires and the sea, it is filled with countless different episodes.

N.º **2050** and **2051,** *The Temptations of St. Anthony,* copies of **Hieronymus Bosch.**

ROOM XLIV.—FLEMISH PRIMITIVES
(Continued.)

This room contains four works by **Albert Dürer** (1471-1528): **N.º 2179,** *Self-portrait* (Plate XXI); **N.º 2180,** *Portrait of an Unknown Man,* and the two nudes, **N.ᵒˢ 2177** and **2178,** *Adam* and *Eve* (Plate 62), all signed with the author's initial. **Dürer** is above all a magnificent draughtsman and colourist, as is attested by his portraits, plethoric with vitality and delicately analysed down to the tiniest detail.

The *Self-portrait* was acquired by Philip IV at the auction of Charles I of England in 1686, and later passed to the Prado Gallery.

The *Portrait of an Unknown Man,* which some identify with Hans Imhoff, is of similar quality to the above; precise in drawing and vigorous in colouring, it represents a man of ruddy complexion and concentrated gaze.

The figures of *Adam* and *Eve,* which were presented to Philip IV by Christina of Sweden and came to the Prado from the Academy of San Fernando, are both very interesting in the history of painting; copies were

made of them, and are now in the Uffizi Gallery at
Florence.

The **N.º 2182** *Portrait of an Old Man*, by **Van Cleve,**
is attributed by others to **Hans Holbein** (1497-1543).
The subject may be Sebastian Munster: this is a work
full of vigour and expression.

N.º 2175 and **2176,** two episodes from the *Hunt in
honour of Charles V at Torgau Castle*, by **Lucas Cranach
«the Elder»** (1472-1553).

N.º 2219, *The Three Graces, or Harmony*, from the royal
collections, a panel by **Hans Baldung** (d. 1545), and
N.º 2220, *The Ages and Death*, by the same.

N.º 2818, *Christ, the Man of Sarrow*, by **Isenbrandt**
(1510-1551).

N.º 2355, *Lady with a yellow carnation*, by a pupil of
François Clouet (French school).

N.º 2100, *St. Jerome*, by **Marinus C. Reymerswaele**
(d. 1567) (Dutch school).

Next, **N.º 2823,** the famous triptych known as the
Garden of Delights or the *Painting of the Madroño* (Plate 63),
filled with the most varied allegories and representations
of sensuality; on the left-hand panel, the Creation; on
the right, Hell; and in the centre, the most extraordinary
types of vegetation, mingled with figures in a veritable
riot which takes place in a wild park of queer plants;
the whole is the fruit of the inflamed imagination of the
Dutch painter **Hieronymus van Aeken Bosch,** known
in Spain as **«el Bosco».**

Lastly, **N.º 2185,** *St. Jerome*, by **Israel van Mecke-
nen,** and **N.º 1541,** *The surgeon*, by **Van Hemesen,** a
picture of good technique, showing several persons in
15th-century dress, attending an operation for extirpation
of the stone of madness.

ROOM XLV.—CENTRAL STAIRCASE

There is not much interest in this staircase which leads to the Lower Floor. On the ceiling is the canvas of the *Death of Absalom*, by **Corrado Giaquinto** (1700-1765), who was in Madrid from 1753 to 1762.

On the wall, two works by **Titian (N.**^{os} **426 and 427)**, *Sisyphus* and *Tityos*, similar themes to those of **Ribera** (1591-1652) which we now come to, namely: **N.º 1113** *Tityos* condemned to be devoured by vultures, and **N.º 1114** *Ixion*, bound to the wheel of torment, both dated 1632 and forming a pair.

At the end of the staircase, **N.º 125,** *The Adoration of the Magis*, and **N.º 126,** *Two Magi Kings*, both by **Pedro Berruguete** (d. 1504).

LOWER FLOOR

ROOM XLVI.—FLEMISH SCHOOL

This room is a passage from the central staircase to the following rooms, and contains several portraits of the Flemish school: **N.º 2569,** *The Infanta Isabel Clara Eugenia*, half-length; **N.º 1499,** *Charles II of England*, at the age of about seven, a replica or copy of **Van Dyck.**
Continuing, **N.º 2526,** *The Earl of Arundel and his grandson Thomas*, and **N.º 2565,** *The Infanta Clara Eugenia*, in widow's weeds; this portrait, like **N.º 2569** just mentioned, are copies of **Van Dyck** from lost originals.

ROOM XLVII

Vestibule of the Paseo del Prado or Velázquez Door entrance. No pictures.

ROOM XLVIII.—GOYA AND BAYEU

Passage leading to the **Goya** section, where we first observe three of his early pictures: **2857,** *Shooting party*,

a «cartoon» for tapestry, and the figures **N.º 2553** and
2554 of *Aesop* and *Menippus*, copied from **Velázquez,**
together with three more cartoons: **N.º 2590,** *The picnic,*
by **Francisco Bayeu** (1734-1795) and **2453,** *Country treat,*
and **2521,** *The «majo» with the guitar,* by Bayeu's brother
Ramón (1746-1793).

ROOM XLIX.—SPANISH PAINTING
OF 15TH AND 16TH CENTURIES

This room contains a series of works, mostly panels
and some of them anonymous, which are followed by
other works, by known continuators of the Spanish primitives.

As we enter the room, on the right side, we see first,
N.º 1040 a, *St. Augustine,* by **J. de la C. Pantoja** (1552-
1608).

Continuing in the same direction we find the following pictures:

N.º 1144, *The Mystical betrothal of St. Catherine,* by
Alonso Sánchez Coello (1531-1588).

N.º 2656, *The Virgin and the Child* (Pl. 88), by **Luis
de Morales** (1500-1586), known as **«el Divino»,** an
Extremaduran painter, a delicaty, highly spiritual artist,
who coincides in many ways with the art of **«el Greco»,**
with Milanese influences. His pictures are very delicate
in detail, filled with a certain religious unction which
the painter perhaps felt deeply, but they are fairly unequal, so that their classification is not easy, since they
include many studio jobs.

N.º 690, *The Nativity,* by **Juan Correa de Vivar,**
who is recorded as having painted for Toledo Cathedral
in 1539.

N.º **2512,** *The Annunciation* and N.º **943,** *The Presentation of the Divine Child* by **Luis de Morales.**

N.º **842,** *Burial of St. Stephen* (Pl. 64) by **Vicente Juan Masip,** more commonly known as **«Juan de Juanes»** (1523?-1579), who introduced the forms of the Italian Renaissance to Valencia, where he did nearly all his work. In his paintings, all on religious subjects and very well known to the general public, influences of **Raphael** and **Leonardo** are to be observed.

N.º **843,** *The Martyrdom of St. Agnes*, by **Juan Vicente Masip** (1475-1550) father and master of **Juan de Juanes.**

N.º **2835,** *The Adoration of the Magis*, by an **anonymous Spaniard** of the Valencian school.

N.º **846,** *The Last Supper*, by **Juan de Juanes** (Plate XXII), a panel painted for the predella of the principal reredos in the Church of San Esteban at Valencia, part of which was also formed by the five panels on the life of that Saint which we shall come to later on the Lower Floor. This picture shows perfect composition of figures, on classic lines, in which we observe a number of heads that are interesting and well drawn, but with a false, artificial colour which gives the appearance of a chromo.

N.º **2834,** *The Nativity* by **anonymous Valencian** and N.º **851,** *The Visitation* by **Juan Masip.**

N.º **838,** *St. Stephen in the Synagogue* by **Juan de Juanes,** is one of the panels he did on themes from the life of St. Stephen for the church of that saint in Valencia.

N.º **689,** *The Visitation* by **J. Correa.**

N.º **2171,** *The Annunciation*, and N.º **2172,** *The Purification*, both by **León Picardo,** painter to the Constable of Castile, at Burgos, between 1514 and 1530.

N.º **2549,** *Miracles of Sts. Cosmas and Damian*, by **Fernando del Rincón,** a Spanish painter of the end of the 15th century.

N.º **687,** *The Presentation of Jesus in the Temple,* by **Juan Correa de Vivar**.

N.º **1256,** *The Adoration of the Magi,* N.º **1258,** *The Circumcision of the Lord,* and N.º **1259,** *The Transitus of the Virgin,* by the **Maestro de la Sisla,** an anonymous Castilian painter of about 1500.

N.º **1290,** *The coronation of the Virgin,* by the artist, known as the **Maestro of the Eleven Thousand Virgins.**

N.º **1298,** *The Descending of the Cross,* by an **anonymous Spaniard.**

Unnumbered, *Christ before Pilate,* **anonymous Hispano-Flemish** of about 1475.

On the opposite wall hang the following pictures.

N.º **2537,** *Christ triumphant,* **anonymous Spaniard,** Castilian, 15th century.

N.º **2517,** *The martyrdom of St. Ursula,* by an **anonymous Hispano-Flemish** artist.

N.º **1329,** *St. Gregory,* and N.º **1331,** *St. James* the *Apostle* by an **anonymous Spaniard**.

N.º **1257,** *The Presentation of the Divine Child* by the **Maestro de la Sisla.**

N.º **2678,** *The Visitation,* a panel by the **Maestro de Perea,** a Valencian of the end of the 15th century.

N.º **1335,** *The Virgin of the Gentleman of Montesa,* author unknown, which may be classified as belonging to the school of **Rodrigo de Osona,** a painter of the end of the 15th century, in whom Flemish and Italian influences are also observable. Represents the **Virgin** with St. Benedict, St. Bernard, and the Gentleman of Montesa, who gives the picture its name, kneeling on the right.

N.º **2682,** *St. Barbara,* **anonymous Spaniard** of about 1520.

N.º **2805,** *St. Anne, the Virgin, St. Elizabeth, St. John and the Child Jesus,* by **Hernando Yáñez de la Alme-**

dina (1505-1536). He introduced Renaissance trends into Spain, being a good pupil of **Leonardo da Vinci,** whose influence is observable in all his works.

N.º 2902, *St. Catherine*, date about 1506, a very careful piece of work, with richness of colouring, by **Hernando Yáñez de la Almedina.** He was a Valencian painter who introduced the first flowering of the Italian Renaissance into Spain. In 1505 he worked beside **Leonardo da Vinci** in his own studio, and became one of his best pupils. The work of **Yáñez** is constantly influenced by **Leonardo's** style, which is recalled by the figures with their classical attitudes and exquisite grace, fine drawing and harmonious colouring, all enhanced by a delicate sensitivity, yet with a grandeur which is very Spanish in its conception.

N.º 3017, *The Descending of the Cross*, by **Pedro Machuca,** a Toledan painter of the 15th. century. This work was purchased by the Prado Trust in 1961.

N.º 2828, *The Annunciation*, by **J. Correa de Vivar.** An important panel for the study of this painter.

N.º 1339, *St. Damian*, a panel in which details and influences of **Leonardo** are observable.

N.º 2579, *Our Lady and the Souls in Purgatory*, by **Pedro Machuca,** a Toledan painter of the 15th century, though he was better as an architect. The work is part of a purchase made for the Prado in Italy in 1935.

N.º 855, *Don Luis de Castellá*, by **Juan de Juanes.** A portrait which is worthy of comparison with any.

N.º 2832, *The apparition of the Virgin to St. Bernard.* A panel by **J. Correa de Vivar.**

N.º 1137, *Isabel Clara Eugenia*, daughter of Philip II and wife of the Archduke Albert, by **A. Sánchez Coello.**

N.º 1030, a copy by **Juan Pantoja de la Cruz** (1553-1608), a pupil of **Sánchez Coello** and also a distin-

guished portraitist, of the portrait of *Isabel de Valois*, third
wife of Philip II, by **Sánchez Coello.**

N.º **2861,** *St. Sebastian between St. Bernard and St. Francis,*
by **Alonso Sánchez-Coello** (1531-1588), one of the
greatest of portrait-painters but less happy in works of
composition.

N.º **1036,** *Portrait of Philip II,* regarded as one of the
best this King, by **A. Sánchez Coello,** a Valencian who
lived from 1531 to 1588, a portraitist of great personality,
fit to figure in any company, and a fine analyst. He
concentrates the whole interest in his subjects' faces; his
works, of excellent technique, make a most interesting
page in the history of the personages of his day.

N.º **1136,** *Prince Carlos,* son of Philip II who saddened
the King's life so greatly, by **A. Sánchez Coello.**

And lastly N.º **1040 b,** *St. Nicholas of Tolentino,* by
J. Pantoja de la Cruz.

ROOM L.—SPANISH RETABLES

For study purposes, Gothic painting in Spain is di-
vided into several schools or regional groups, which
we may reduce to two: the Andalusian and the Castilian.

This room contains two such retable, both of high
merit, together with fragments of others. The whole set
can be assigned to the cycle of **Berruguete** and **Fernando Gallego.**

N.º **1321,** the so-called *Retable of Archbishop Sancho
de Rojas.* It comes from the Monastery of San Benito at
Valladolid, and was done in the first quarter of the 15th
century by an **anonymous Spaniard.**

N.º **1324,** *St. Sebastian and St. Polycarp,* and N.º **1325,**

**Autorretrato.—Self-portrait du peintre par lui même.—Sebstbildnis.
Autoritratto**

La última Cena.—Last Supper.—La dernière Cène.—Das heilige Abendmahl.—L'ultima Cena

Martyrdom of Sts. Sebastian and Polycarp, panels attributed to **Pedro García de Benabarre,** a painter of the Spanish of whom nothing is known except that he worked during the years 1455 and 1456.

Two panels, **N.**os **2670** and **2671,** on themes of the *Martyrdom of St. Vicent*, by an **anonymous Spaniard.** From the Bosch Bequest.

N.o **2680,** *The Crucifixion*, by a pupil of **Jaume Huguet.**

N.o **1334,** *St. Vincent, Deacon and Martyr*, anonymous panel of the Aragonese cycle, which coincides in essential respects with the work of the **Maestro del Arzobispado Dalmau de Mur,** of the last quarter of the 15th century. From the *Seo* (Cathedral) of Saragossa, whence it went to the Archaeological Museum, and finally to the Prado.

N.o **2668,** *Translation of the body of St. James the Greater, I. Embarkation at Jaffa;* in the background, Herod with his suite witnessing the embarkation of the beheaded body of the Apostle, while the executioner sheaths his sword.

N.o **2669,** *Translation of the body of St. James the Greater, II. Its conveyance in Galicia*. Both panels are well preserved and attractively coloured. They must have formed part of a retable of the Aragonese school. The unknown author is identified by some with the **Maestro de Aljafarín.**

N.o **2545,** *Retable of the life of the Virgin and St. Francis of Assisi*. From the province of León. The artist is **Nicolás Francés** (d. 1468); all we known of him is that he was painting in León before 1434. This artist shows affectations in his work and is influenced by Italian trends.

Beside this retable is another of five panels, which may have formed part of the Chapel of the Arces in Sigüenza Cathedral. The best of all is the central one, which gives its name to retable **N.º 1336,** *St. John the Baptist and St. Catherine* (Plate 66), a harmonious and very beautiful panel, with delicate colour qualities. It is by an anonymous Castilian-Aragonese author, whom some identify with the **Maestro de Sigüenza,** belonging to the second half of the 15th century.

Lastly, an altar panel, **N.º 1332,** from a reredos at Argüis (Huesca), based on the *Legend of St. Michael.* It is attributed to the **Maestro de Argüis,** who must have done it in the middle of the 15th century. It came to the Prado the Archaeological Museum.

ROOM LI.—ROTUNDA ROMANESQUE PAINTING

On the walls of this vestibule hang eight battlepieces by **Snayers** (1592-1667, Flemish school); but the most interesting thing here is the small Romanesque chapel, reconstructed on one of the two sides of the room, with the wall-paintings of the *ermita* (hermitage, chapel) of La Cruz at Maderuelo (Segovia), transferred from their site to this Gallery, where they can be examined as an important specimen of 12th-century art. The chapel is profusely decorated on its walls and ceiling, although important pieces are missing here and there.

First, in the entance, we see a well-preserved scene: *The first sin* and *The Creation of Adam* (Plate 67). In the apse, *Christ the Creator of Pantocrator;* the entire chapel is adorned with figures of angels, prophets and saints.

ROOM LII

A small gallery between the Rotunda and the Lower North Door. It contains six works by **Anibale Carracci** (1560-1609), of Bologna and belonging to a family of painters, Agostino, Giovanni Antonio and Anibale, the last-named being much the best. Lastly, there is a fresco, **N.º 2911,** *St. John the Evangelist*, by **Antonio Mohedano,** a Spanish painter who died at Cordoba in 1625.

ROOM LIII.—GOYA, DRAWINGS

This Room is entirely given over to the important collection of **Goya's** drawings (Plates 68 and 69). Some of those in this Room came to the Prado from the Museum of La Trinidad when it was closed; others were bought from private persons by the Prado Trust. They are, as a rule, rough sketches made without a model in quick, free strokes, and nearly all are jottings for the painter's series of engravings. **Goya** was not a man of much education, but he had an amazing intuitive power of masterign his figures and giving them life. Here we see his extensive drawing work, in sketches traced with a steady hand in sure lines; crude and daring, they sometimes lash the vices of society of the day with allusions or satires of moral or political type, aimed at the excessive liberties of priets, friars and rulers. The quality of the drawings is extraordinary, and supplements the robust personality of this genuine master of Spanish art, whose enormous output of works is only equalled by their amazing variety of techniques and themes.

ROOM LIV.—GOYA, PAINTINGS

We may begin with **N.º 738,** *Cardinal Don Luis María de Borbón,* and **N.º 740 B,** *Queen María Luisa,* a more than half-length portrait, in low-necked dress and with plumed headdress.

Religious painting is not Goya's strong suit, and his works on such subjects succeed only occasionally, as in *The Communion of St. Joseph Calasanctius,* in the Convent of San Antón, Madrid.

Here we see **N.º 745,** his *Christ crucified,* dated 1780 and belonging to his first period. It is perfectly painted, and the modelling of the nude is notable, as is the fine quality of the colour, with Italian influences observable; but there is no religious feeling. Note that Christ is shown crucified with four nails, in the French manner.

This picture, which was done for Goya's admission into the San Fernando Academy of Fine Arts, comes from the church of San Francisco el Grande.

N.º 740 a, *Charles IV,* more than half-length portrait showing the King dressed in red with the Golden Fleece and the ribbon of Charles III.

N.º 746, *The Holy Family,* a juvenile work, hence the influence of **Mengs** can be seen.

N.º 2447, Doña María Antonia Gonzaga, *Marquesa de Villafranca.*

N.º 739, *The Duke and Duchess of Osuna and their children,* presented to the Prado by their descendants.

N.º 2446, *Cornelius van der Gotten,* sometime director of the Royal Tapestry Factory, painted in 1782.

N.º 2862, *Queen Maria Luisa with hoop skirt.* In this 17th-century mode, and with big hat.

ROOM LV.—GOYA, CARTOONS
FOR TAPESTRIS

These three consecutive Rooms display the important collection of «cartoons» for tapestries to be woven in the Royal Factory.

The canvases are perfectly placed on the walls and offer us one of the best series in the Gallery. In **Goya's** first period, on his return from Italy, he was commissioned to paint, for the Royal Tapestry Factory, the cartoons depicting the model to be afterwards done in tapestry. He came with a recommendation from **Rafael Mengs,** and here he began the first stage of his art, which is very interesting, original and beautiful, though not the best of his career. From 1775 to 1791 he turned out paintings for tapestries which went to adorn the royal residences and which are notable for both numbers and variety. Here the painter begins a new phase of his art, in which he steadily develops and surpasses himself till he attains some truly admirable ensembles. He puts his vigorous temperament into the work, and this was to open up new avenues to him in his profession. He introduced a change in the technique of tapestrym and, adapting himselt the exigencies of fabric with its few colours, he produced cartoons full of a luminous, vivid and really surprising colour. They are very much after the taste of the period, but with a sense of refinement, these popular scenes of picnics, games and dances by the banks of a river; the artist moves his figures with grace, and achieves good compositions and marvellous effects of light and colour.

We first see **N.º 778,** *The blind man with the guitar;* **N.º 779,** *Madrid Fair;* **N.º 771,** *The «maja» and the muffled men;* **N.º 805,** *Sportsman with dogs;* **N.º 795,** *The vintage;*

N.º **787,** *The fight with young bulls;* **N.º 784,** *The game of pelota;* **N.º 772,** *The drinker;* **N.º 800,** *The girls with pitchers;* **N.º 773,** *The sunshade;* **N.º 753,** *Dogs and hunting gear;* and **N.º 792,** *The appointment.*

ROOM LV A.—GOYA, HISTORICAL PICTURES AND PORTRAITS

Besides being an admirable portrait-painter, **Francisco de Goya** excels in historical themes, with these episodes throbbing with the popular heroism of the war of 1808. The Spaniards, in guerrilla bands, fight fiercely against the Napoleonic invasion; the call to arms flies from end to end of the Peninsula, as the people, with unwonted heroism, gradually throws back the invader. The painter saw these scenes himself, his patriotic spirit was stirred, and he has left us these superb creations, which in themselves form one of the best pages in history.

N.º 748, *The Second of May in Madrid: the battle with the Mamelukes* (Plate XXIV), and **N.º 749,** scenes from *The Third of May 1808 in Madrid: The shootings on the Hill of Príncipe Pío* (Plate 70). In the first picture, civilians and Mamelukes, in a confused turmoil, slash ferociously at one another; the second picture, that of the shootings, is also full of astonishing realism. In the middle, an anonymous hero with his arms outstretched, a true symbol of the popular outcry, defies the firing-squad, while the others hide their horrified eyes from the tragedy being consummated; on the other side, a pile of corpses in a pool of blood; the whole in the darkness of night, illuminated only by the lamplight, which further accentuates the livid contrasts.

N.º **724,** portrait of *Ferdinand VII in a camp*, like the other here with some technical successes, but painted with some apathy and indifference.

N.º **723,** *Self-portrait* (Plate XXIII), magnificent, and perfect in light and colour.

N.º **747,** *The exorcized man*, a fine picture which shows the religious rite of expelling the devils from the possessed man who is seen in the centre, held by a woman, while the priest sprinkles him with holy water.

N.º **740 I,** *The beheading*, repetition of another panel; **N.**º **2650,** *St. Justa and St. Rufina*, a sketch for the picture in Seville Cathedral.

N.º **740 J,** *The bonfire*, painted on tinplate like **740 I.**

N.º **2899,** *The milk-woman of Bordeaux*, regarded as **Goya's** last painting; a canvas executed with fine delicate brushwork, delightful in colouring, with impressionist details which place him among the most modern artists, and far ahead of his time in this modality of art.

N.º **725,** *General Palafox on horseback*, a picture in which we note blackening of the shadows. The general's figure is moderately good only; the best feature is regarded as being the head, with marked and vigorous strokes.

N.º **2898,** *Don Juan Bautista de Muguiro*, a portrait with dedication by his friend the painter.

Lastly, **N.**º **735,** *Ferdinand VII in royal mantle*.

ROOM LVI.—GOYA, TAPESTRY CARTOONS
(Continued.)

N.º **781,** *The officer and the lady;* **N.**º **804,** *Blind man's buff*, beautiful and perfect in every respect and regarded

as one of the finest he ever did; **N.º 782,** *The haw-seller;*
N.º 768, *Picnic beside the Manzanares;* **N.º 794,** *The threshing-floor;* **N.º 769,** *Dance near the Chapel of San Antonio de la Florida;* **N.º 797,** *Poor people at the fountain;* **N.º 798,** *The snowstorm;* **N.º 796,** *The injured bricklayer;* **N.º 777,** *Boys picking fruit;* **N.º 790,** *The boy with the linnet;* **N.º 788,** *The tobacco excise service;* **N.º 770,** *Brawl at the New Inn;* **N.º 775,** *Card-players;* **N.º 789,** *The little boy and the tree,* and **N.º 776,** *Children blowing up a bladder.*

ROOM LVI A.—GOYA «BLACK PAINTINGS»

The superb portraits in greys and the scenes of the Second of May are followed by this disconcerting art done in hard swipes of the big brush. Old, practically stone-deaf, living alone in his house known as «Deaf Man's Lodge» on the bank of the Manzánares, Goya covered its walls with paintings on weird, uncanny themes, revealing a tormented mind. They were done in oil, and this made it possible for them to be removed and to remain on view today. The basis is black or grey, with an occasional touch of dull red: «The slumber of reason begets monsters»; the painter's artistic imagination runs riot and breaks with every formula till it arrives at the most advanced traits of the contemporary. Great strokes, scrapes with the paletteknife, disorderly splodges of the big brush, bring out surprising effects of light, now stressing cheekbones, now noses.

Here we see fourteen of these interesting works: sabbaths, donkeys, flying witches, hooded figures, «manolas», monsters, soldiers, strumpets, friars and billy-goats, a queer decoration for the dining-room and sitting-room of the painter's house.

El Salvador.—The Saviour.—Le Sauveur.—Der Erlöser.—Il Salvatore

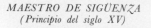

Retablo de San Juan Bautista y Santa Catalina.—Reredos of Sain John and Saint Catherine.—Retable de Saint-Jean-Baptiste et Sainte-Catherine.—Altarblatt des Johannes de Täufer un die Heilige Katharina. S. Giovanni Battista e S. Caterina (dipinto su legno per altare)

La creación de Adán. El pecado original.—The Creation of Adam. The original sin.—La création d'Adam. Le
peché original.—Die Erbsünde und die Erschaffung Adams.—La creazione di Adamo ed il peccato originale

Dibujo.—A drawing.—Dessin.—Zeichnung.—Disegno

«Esto ya se ve» (dibujo).—«This can be seen» (drawing).—«Già si vede ciò»

Los fusilamientos del 3 de Mayo de 1808.—Fusillade of the 3rd May 1808.—La Fusillade de 3 Mai 1808.
Die Erschiessung am 3 May 1808.—Le fucilazioni del 3 Maggio 1808

Saturno devorando a sus hijos.—Saturn devouring his children.—Saturne dévorant ses enfants.—Saturno verschlingt seine Kinder.—Saturno mentre divora i suoi figli

Arte helenístico.—Hellenistic Art.—Art Hellénistique.—Griechische Kunst.—Arte ellenistica

LÁM. 72

Arte helenistico.—Hellenistic Art.—Art Hellénistique.—Griechiscne
Hunst.—Arte ellenistica

**María Tudor, esposa de Felipe II.—Mary Tudor, Queen of England.
Marie Tudor Reine d'Angleterre.—Die Königin Maria von England.
Maria Tudor, sposa di Filippo II**

**El cambista y su mujer.—The Moneychanger and his wife.—Le Chan-
geur et sa femme.—Der Geldwechsler und seine Frau.—Il Cambiavalute
e sua moglie**

Dama y niña.—Lady and Child.—Dame et son enfant.—Dame und Kind.
Dama con una bambina

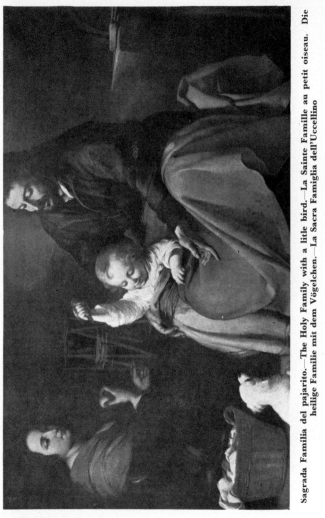

Sagrada Familia del pajarito.—The Holy Family with a litle bird.—La Sainte Famille au petit oiseau. Die heilige Familie mit dem Vögelchen.—La Sacra Famiglia dell'Uccellino

Santa Ana y la Virgen.—Saint Anne and the Virgin.—Sainte-Anne et la Vierge.—Die Heilige Anna und die Heilige Jungfrau.—S. Anna e la Madonna

Rebeca y Eliecer. — Rebeca and Eliecer. — Rebeca et Eliecer. — Rebekka und Eliese. — Rebecca ed Eliezero

La Adoración de los pastores (fragmento).—The Adoration of the Shepherds (fragment).—L'Adoration des bergers.—Die Anbetung der Hirten. L'Adorazione dei Pastori

N.º **766,** *The reading;* **N.**º **760,** *The pilgrimage of San Isidro;* **N.**º 757, *Destiny;* **N.**º **756,** *Witches' sabbath;* **N.**º **759,** *Two old friars;* **N.**º **755,** *Pilgrimage to the fountain of San Isidro;* **N.**º **758,** *Fight with cudgels;* **N.**º **761,** *Fantastic vision;* **N.**º **765,** *Two women laughing and a man;* **N.**º **762,** *Old men eating soup;* **N.**º **764,** *Judith and Holofernes;* **N.**º **754,** *A «manola»;* **N.**º **763,** *Saturn devouring one of his children* (Plate 71); **N.**º **767,** *Dog buried in the sand.*

These unparallelled works, the fruit of a prodigious character and genius, belonged in 1873 to the German banker Emile d'Erlanger, who commissioned their transfer onto canvas. They were shown at the Paris World Exhibition of 1878, and were finally donated by their owner to the Prado.

ROOM LVII.—GOYA, TAPESTRY CARTOONS
(Continued.)

N.º **801,** *The stilts;* **N.**º **774,** *The kite;* **N.**º **786,** *The washerwomen;* **N.**º **802,** *The dummy,* some boys tossing a doll in a blanket; **N.**º **785,** *The swing;* **N.**º **793,** *Flower girls;* **N.**º **799,** *The wedding;* **N.**º **780,** *The crockseller;* **N.**º **783,** *Boys playing at soldiers;* **N.**º **800,** *The Giants;* **N.**º **791,** *The woodcutters;* **N.**º **803,** *Boys climbing a tree;* and **N.**º **743,** *The «majo» with the guitar.*

ROOM LVII A.—GOYA, PAINTINGS
AND CARTOONS

In this room, beside tapestry cartoons and other paintings, we see some beautiful small-sized paintings, of «cabinet» type, which were done for the Alameda of the Duke and Duchess of Osuna.

N.º 728, *Queen María Luisa*, full length, in black «maja» dress with mantilla and fan.

N.º 2785, *The colossus, or Panic*. Almost the whole canvas is occupied by a giant, from whom the terrified crowd flees from one side to another; only a donkey reamains unmoved.

N.º 727, *Charles IV*, in the uniform of a colonel of Life Guards, with his hat in his left hand.

N.º 751, *A dead turkey*, and **N.º 752,** *Dead birds*.

N.º 2782, *Drunken bricklayer*, a sketch of reduced size from the tapestry-cartoon *The injured bricklayer*, with only the expressions of the figures altered.

N.º 2895, *The flageolet-player*, a tapestry-cartoon which matches **N.º 2896,** *Sportsman beside a fountain*, hanging on the same wall.

N.º 2781, *Blind man's buff*, a smaller variant of the other of the same title which we have already seen, done for the Alameda de Osuna.

N.º 750, *The Meadow of San Isidro on the Saint's Day*, a view of this meadow with a motley popular assembly, playing and amusing themselves on the banks of the Manzanares; in the background, Madrid, with the Royal Palace and the church of San Francisco el Grande conspicuous. Study for a tapestry which was never woven. Belonged to the Ducal House of Osuna.

N.º 2783, *The Chapel of San Isidro on the Saint's Day*. «Majos» and «majas» drinking from the miraculous spring. Related, like the foregoing, to a tapestry-cartoon.

N.º 744, *A picador*. On horseback, with short country dress and «montera» hat.

N.º 2856, *Fowling with decoy*, and **N.º 2524,** *Two children with a dog*, both tapestry-cartoons.

ROOM LVIII.—SCULPTURE

The world-wide fame of the Prado Gallery undoubtedly rest on its collections of pictures; in addition, however, it contains a variety of works of sculpture, some of which are unique specimens. Most of the sculptures are assembled in Rooms LVIII and LXXI on the Lower Floor; others are distributed among the different rooms and halls of the Gallery, thus contributing to the decoration. Nearly all come from the Royal Collections. We note first and foremost those from the collection of Isabel de Farnesio, wife of Philip V and a great *amateur* of works of art, of which she amassed a large quantity. She sent her agents to Italy to acquire the sculptures that had belonged to Cristina of Sweden and were sold in Rome, the series of statues of Charles V and Philip II, notably those sent by Pope Paul III to Charles V and those sent by Cardinal Montepulciano to Philip II.

A group of sculptures assigned to the Hispano-Roman period, for the most part Roman copies of Greek models, in which some variants are to be seen. The most notable are: *The archaic Apollo*, from the Zayas bequest, and the group of *Castor and Pollux*, one of the best known in the artistic world. It was found at Rome in the 16th century and belonged to the House of Ludovisi, then to Christina of Sweden, and then to King Philip V and Queen Isabel de Farnesio. After being in the Palace of La Granja for a time it finally passed to the Prado, This marble group is classified as of Greek type, by an unknown author later than Polycletus and Praxiteles.

Venus, rather mutilated, from the Zayas bequest.

The faun with the kid, of the same period, an unfinished figure showing affinities to the school of **Rhodes.**

Aphrodite, from the same bequest. The *Venus* of the

Dauphin, resembling those in the Capitol at Rome and that of the Medici at Florence. This one is regarded as one of the finest and most interesting.

A faun, copy of an original by Praxiteles.

Polymnia, copy of a Greek original of the Hellenistic period.

Hypnos, of the 4th century B. C

Venus after the bath, *Ganymede and the eagle*, the figures of the *Diadumenos*, *Isis*, *Euterpe*, *Thalia*, *Calliope*, *Terpsichore*, and the marble reliefs of some *Bacchantes*, from the Isabel de Farnesio collection.

A large group of Roman busts purchased at Rome and Tivoli by the Spanish ambassador D. Nicolás de Azara, who presented them to Charles IV: *Alexander the Great*, *Pericles*, *Mark Antony*, *Antinous*, *Cicero* and those of *Augustus Caesar*. Another lesser group besides those purchased by **Velázquez** on instructions from Philip IV during his 1648 visit to Italy; some marble reliefs and figures of animals.

ROOM LIX.—FLEMISH PAINTINGS OF THE 16TH CENTURY

This is a collection of works by Flemish and German painters, as a continuation of the primitives we saw on the main floor.

By **Ambrosius Benson** (1519-1550), there is a series of panels on religious themes, from the Convent of Santa Cruz at Segovia:

N.º 1929, *The Nativity of Our Lady;* **N.º 1927,** *Pietà;* **N.º 1303,** *St. Dominic Guzmán;* **N.º 1304,** *St. Thomas* (?) *and a donor;* **N.º 1928,** *The burial of Christ;* **N.º 1935,** *The embrace before the golden gate;* and **N.º 1933,** *St. Anne, the Child Jesus and the Virgin*.

N.º 1296, *Zachary.* Leaf of a polyptych in which the Patriarch is depicted with an expression of astonishment. On the other side of the panel *St. Bernardine of Siena* is depicted. A work by **Jan Prevost** or **Provost** (1465-1529). Flemish school.

N.º 2183, *The Augsburg goldsmith Jörg Zörer,* and **N.º 2184,** *The wife of Jörg Zörer,* both figures half-length, by **Christoph Amberger** (1500-1562); they came from the Royal Palace at Aranjuez.

N.º 2539, *Pietà,* by the **Flemish Maestro of the Virgo inter Virgines.**

N.º 2552, a triptych. Centre: *Nativity;* on the doorleaves, *The Annunciation* and *The Presentation in the Temple,* by an **anonymous Fleming** of the middle 16th century, known as the **Maestro de las Medias Figuras.**

N.º 2217, *Triptych of the Adoration of the Magis,* by an **anonymous Fleming** of the beginning of the 16th century.

N.º 2703, *The Annunciation,* triptych by **Pieter Coecke van Aelst** (1502-1550).

N.º 2706, *Betrothal of the Virgin,* leaf of a triptych, by an **anonymous Fleming** of about 1520, known as the **Maestro de la Leyenda de Santa Catalina.**

N.º 1916, *Mystical betrothal of St. Catherine,* triptych by an **anonymous Fleming** of abut 1520.

N.º 2697, *St. Jerome,* panel by the Dutchman **Van Oostsanen** (1470-1533).

N.º 1917, *Miracle at Toulouse of St. Anthony of Padua,* panel by an **anonymous Fleming** of about 1500.

ROOM LX.—PORTRAITS BY ANTONIO MORO AND OTHERS

Anton van Dashorst Mor, known in Spain as **Antonio Moro** (1519?-1576), a Dutchman, was a master in the art of portraiture, and greatly admire by Philip II, in whose service he was. Here we have a series of Court portraits, magnificent and well composed, full of dignity and very detailed.

N.º 2112, Princess *Doña Juana de Austria*, mother of King Sebastian of Portugal and daughter of the Emperor Charles V; **N.º 2109,** *Doña Catalina de Austria*, wife of John III of Portugal and sister of Charles V; **N.º 2107,** *Pejerón*, buffoon to the Count of Benavente and the great Duke of Alba; **N.º 2114,** *Metgen*, the painter's wife; **N.º 2116,** *Lady with cross hanging at her neck*, unidentified portrait; **N.º 2117 bis,** *Doña María Josefa de Portugal*, wife of Alejandro Farnesio, a small portrait making a pair with **N.º 2117,** *Margarita of Parma*, Charles V's daughter; **N.º 2118,** *Philip II*, youthful portrait of the King, small size; **N.º 2115,** *The Duchess of Feria* (?), Juana Dormer, a great friend of Mary Tudor; **N.º 2110,** *The Empress Doña María of Austria*, wife of Maximilian II and daughter of Charles V; **N.º 2108,** *Queen Mary of England* (Plate 74), Mary Tudor, second wife of Philip II, daughter of Henry VIII and Catherine of Aragon; **N.º 2111,** *The Emperor Maximilian II*, a companion picture to **N.º 2110** of his wife; **N.º 2119,** *The lady with the gold chains*, unidentified; **N.º 2113,** *Lady with the jewel*, whom it has been thought to identify with Doña María of Portugal, betrothed wife of Philip II, and **N.º 2880,** *Portrait of a lady*.

N.º 1949, *Philip II*. Portrait, by **Lucas de Heere** (?) (1534-1584). Dutch school.

N.º **2580,** *A humanist*, by **Jan van Scorel** (1495-1562).

N.º **2567,** *The money-changer and his wife* (Plate 75), by **Marinus Claeszon van Reymerswaele** (d. 1567), Dutch school. The types are well done as regards drawing, but not in quality of colour.

ROOM LX A.—FLEMISH PAINTERS
OF THE 16TH CENTURY

We begin with **N.º 2884,** *Judith with the head of Holofernes*, by an **anonymous Fleming** of the 15th century.

N.ºs 2074 and **2075,** *Dutch Lady and little girl* (Plate 76); **N.º 2076,** portrait of a *Dutch lady*, and **N.º 2073,** *Lady with a yellow flower*, all by **A. Cronenburch,** of the Dutch school, last third of 16th century.

The triptych **N.ºs 1468, 1469** and **1470,** *The life of the Virgin*, with her Birth, Presentation and Transitus, by **M. Coxyen** (1499-1592).

N.º 1515, *The Universal Flood*, by **J. van Scorel** (1495-1562).

N.º 2101, *The Virgin and Child*, by **M. van Reymerswaele,** Dutch painter of the end of the 15th century.

On either side, the portraits **N.º 1858,** *Don Alonso de Idiáquez, Duke of Ciudad Real*, and **N.º 1859,** *Doña Juana de Robles*, wife of the foregoing, painted by **Otto van Veen** (1558-1629), Flemish school.

N.º 1542, *The Virgin and Child*, by **Van Hemesen,** dated 1543.

N.º 1960, portrait of a gentleman, by an **anonymous Dutchman** of about 1568.

N.º 2881, *Portrait of a young man*, by a pupil of **Antonio Moro.**

Lastly, **N.º 2641,** *Christ with the Cross,* by **Michael Coxcie** (1499-1592), and **N.º 2100,** *St. Jerome,* by **Marinus van Reymerswaele,** signed in 1517.

ROOM LXI.—MURILLO

Our attention is strongly drawn to the oblong picture **N.º 960,** *The Holy Family,* commonly known as the Holy Family *of the Little Bird* (Plate 77), which is dated 1650 and belonged to the Isabel de Farnesio collection. It was carried off to France during the general looting of works of art under José Buonaparte, and was returned in 1918; it is a family scene full of innocence and charm.

N.º 977, *Our Lady of Sorrows,* and **N.º 965,** *Ecce-Homo,* both purchased by Charles IV for the Aranjuez Palace; **N.º 968,** *St. Anne and the Virgin* (Plate 78); **N.º 975,** *Our Lady of the Rosary;* **N.º 996,** *Rebecca and Eliezer* (Plate 79); **N.º 961,** *The Adoration of the Shepherds* (Plate 80), a picture of harmonious colouring and good arrangement of figures; **N.º 973,** *The Immaculate Conception,* half-length, a theme which **Murillo** had a special preference for and painted several times; **N.º 969,** *The Annunciation;* **N.º 982,** *The martyrdom of St. Andrew;* **N.º 976,** *The Virgin with the Child;* **N.º 981,** *Vision of St. Francis;* **N.º 1001,** *Old woman spinning;* **N.º 1002,** *The Galician woman with the coin,* from the Isabel de Farnesio collection; **N.º 987,** *St. Jerome;* **N.º 983,** *St. Ferdinand,* and two pictures of *Christ on the Cross,* **N.ᵒˢ 966** and **967.**

**Autorretrato.—Self portrait.—Portrait par lui-même.—Selbstbildnis.
Autoritratto**

Los Mamelucos

ROOM LXI A.—RIBERA

By the Valencian **José de Ribera,** known as **«el Españoleto»,** an artist who is outstanding in the technique of chiaroscuro, and continuing his work, we here have the following pictures:

N.º **1107,** *Vision of St. Francis of Assisi.*

N.º **1124,** *Fight between women,* a strange picture dated 1636, which draws one's attention; it is based on a duel which took place at Naples and was witnessed by the Marqués de Vasto, and in which the Italian women Isabella de Carazzi and Diambra de Petinella fought for the love of Fabio de Zaresola.

More in keeping with the genius of **Ribera** are the religious themes of this whole series of saints and scenes of their martyrdom, of which we have seen some, such as the following:

N.º **1115,** *St. Paul the Hermit;* N.º **1120,** *Aesop,* writing; N.º **1098,** *St. Jerome, penitent,* naked; in his right and, a stone with which he strikes his breast, in his left a cross.

N.º **1091,** *St. Simon;* N.º **1082,** *St. James the Greater,* with red mantle and pilgrim's staff in right hand, rather less than half-length.

N.º **1095,** *St. Sebastian,* showing the saint half-length, with a good study of figure modelling, on which account **Velázquez** esteemed the picture highly.

N.º **1094,** *St. Augustine in prayer;* N.º **1102,** *St. Joseph and the Child Jesus;* N.º **1123,** *Head of old man,* representing Bacchus, which, with N.º **1122,** *Head of woman,* profile, are fragments of picture entitled *The Triumph of Bacchus,* which got burnt in the fire of the Alcázar in 1734.

N.º **1110,** *St. Roch;* N.º **1121,** *Archimedes with the compass;* N.º **1112,** *The blind Gambazo,* a sculptor, feeling a head of Apollo; N.º **1073,** *St. Peter «in Vinculis»;* N.º

1079, *St. Andrew;* **N.º 1116,** *An anchorite,* with cross in left hand; **N.º 1071,** *St. Peter;* **N.º 1070,** *The Immaculate Conception,* **N.º 1077,** *St. Andrew;* and **N.º 1111,** *St. Christopher.*

ROOM LXII.—MURILLO AND OTHERS

In the first place we see copies of two *self-portraits* by **Bartolomé Esteban Murillo; N.º 2912,** anonymous, and **N.º 1153,** somewhat smaller than the original, the property of Earl Spencer, by **M. de Tobar** (1678-1758).

Four small sketches by **Murillo** (1618-1682) on the parable of the Prodigal Son; **N.º 997,** *The prodigal son receives his portion;* his father hands him the money in bags; **N.º 998,** *The farewell;* he rides out of the town; **N.º 999,** *Dissipation;* table with viands, two courtesans and a musician; **N.º 1000,** *Abandonment;* poor, alone in the fields, amid swine.

N.º 989, *St. James the Apostle,* more than half-length, also by **Murillo,** who is likewise the author of **N.ºˢ 1005** and **1006,** two landscapes making a pair.

N.º 1160, *The Presentation of the Virgin in the Temple,* by **Juan de Valdés Leal** (1622-1690). At the foot of the stairs, with St. Joachim and St. Anne, there are other figures; the one holding a ewer is thought to be a self-portrait.

N.º 970, *The Annunciation,* and **N.º 996 a,** *Christ and the Samaritan woman,* both by **Murillo.**

The Guipuzcoan artist **Ignacio Iriarte** (1621-1685) is the author of **N.º 2970,** *Landscape with shepherds,* and **N.º 836,** *Country.*

N.º 2509, *The Rich Man and the beggar Lazarus,* scene of the parable, by **Juan de Sevilla** (1643-1695), a contemporary of **Murillo** who follows the Baroque trend of **Rubens.**

Lastly, **N.º 984,** *The conversion of St. Paul,* by **Murillo.** Christ appears to Saul, who has fallen off his horse, and asks him «Why persecutest thou me?».

ROOM LXII A.—RIBERA AND ZURBARAN

Here we have **Ribera's** pictures again:

N.º 1090, *St. Simon;* **N.º 1099,** *St. Bartholomew;* **N.º 1096,** *St. Jerome* (Plate 81), half-length, the torso half nude, with hands crossed over chest; **N.º 2506,** *Old woman usurer,* canvas dated (left hand bottom corner) 1638; **N.º 1104,** *The penitent Magdalene,* half-length, with a skull and a flask of perfume; **N.º 1084,** *St. Matthew;* **N.º 1067,** *The Saviour.*

N.º 1089, *St. James the Less;* **N.º 1092,** *St. Judas Thaddaeus;* **N.º 1074,** *St. Paul;* **N.º 1888,** *St. Philip;* and finally two pictures by **Zurbarán, N.º 3009,** *Friar Diego de Vega;* **N.º 3006,** *St. Claire.*

ROOM LXIII.—ALONSO CANO AND CARREÑO DE MIRANDA

Alonso Cano was born at Granada in 1601 and died there in 1667. He is one of the great masters of the 17th century; architect, painter and sculptor, a principal figure in Granada art, he was firts and foremost an architect. He possessed an ample sense of beauty, which makes it possible to compare him with, and even make him a rival to, the great figures of the Renaissance. His pictures —extraordinarily beautiful, in a serene, classical line, well executed with perfect drawing and delicate colouring— show the excellence of this Granadan artist and author of reredoses, which he executed in their entirety, drawing the architectural plans, painting the pictures and carving the statues. His most notable work is the set of pictures he did for the chancel of Granada Cathedral. The Prado contains only a very few of his works, from which it is hardly possible to study him properly. Here are six on religious themes.

N.º 629, *The deand Christ sustained by un angel,* and **N.º 2637,** repetition of the same with some variants. The first belonged to the Marqués de la Ensenada and comes from the Madrid Royal Palace; the latter, signed on the stone which supports the figure of Christ, comes from the Bosch Bequest.

N.º 625, *St. Benedict* contemplating the globe and three angels; **N.º 630,** *The Virgin contemplating her Divine Son* (Plate 82); above the head of Mary, a bright star; **N.º 626,** *St. Jerome,* listening to the trump that announces the Last Judgement; **N.º 627,** *The Virgin and the Child,* very similar to **N.º 630,** and lastly **N.º 632,** *A King of León.*

Juan Carreño de Miranda was born at Avilés in 1614 and died in Madrid in 1685. He is one of the so-called minor masters of the Madrid School, a portraitist of Charles II's court, a good painter who studies **Velázquez** a great deal. Here we see some religious works of his, very delicate and well achieved, and showing Flemish influences: **N.º 651,** *St. Anne and the Virgin,* and **N.º 649,** *St. Sebastian.*

N.º 647, *The buffoon Francisco Bazán,* full-length portrait; **N.º 645,** *Peter Ivanovitz Potemkin,* who was twice Russian Ambassador in Madrid, in 1668 and 1681; **N.º 646,** *Eugenia Martínez Vallejo «the Monster»,* an abnormal girl of five years, clothed, by **Juan Carreño** *de*

Miranda (1614-1685), who also painted her nude as Bacchus crowned with vine-clusters, **N.º 2800,** «*The Monster*» *nude*.

ROOM LXIII A.—ANTONIO DEL CASTILLO,
FRAY JUAN RIZI AND OTHERS

Antonio del Castillo (1603-1668) is a good painter from Cordova, a pupil of **Zurbarán's** and artist of solid brushwork and firm draughtsmanship.

Here we see six pictures of his on passages from the life of Joseph: **N.º 951,** *Joseph and his brethren;* **N.º 952,** *Joseph sold by his brethren;* **N.º 953,** *Joseph and Potiphar's wife;* **N.º 954,** *Joseph explains Pharaoh's dreams;* **N.º 955,** *The triumph of Joseph in Egypt,* and **N.º 956,** *Joseph orders the detention of Simeon*.

Esteban March (d. 1660), a Valencian painter, who followed in the footsteps of **Ribera** rather unsuccessfully. By him we have **N.º 878,** *Old drinker;* **N.º 882,** *St. Onuphrius,* and **879,** *Old woman drinker,* with a bottle in her hand.

ROOM LXIV.—SPANISH PAINTERS
OF THE 17TH CENTURY

First, **N.º 648,** *Charles II,* son of Philip IV, by **Juan Carreño de Miranda** (1614-1685), and another of the same, **N.º 2504,** by **Claudio Coello** (1642-1693).

N.º 2571, *The Hunt of the Tabladillo* (Plate 84), at Aranjuez, by **Mazo** (d. 1667). Queen Isabella and ladies of the Court, seated on the platform; Philip IV, Don Fernando and two huntsmen in front of two stags, inside the stockade; outside it, several groups of people on foot and on horseback; in foreground, right, beside a negro buffoon, the dog that **Velázquez** painted with Don Antonio «el Inglés».

N.º 888, *The Empress Margarita of Austria*, daughter of Philip IV, who was painted as a child by **Velázquez** in *Las Meninas*, and **N.º 1221,** *Prince Baltasar Carlos*, both by **Mazo.**

N.º 2244, *St. Augustine*, kneeling, contemplates the apparition of the Virgin with the Child; signed in 1663 by **Mateo Cerezo** (1626-1666).

N.º 2505, *A son of Francisco Ramos del Manzano*, as a child of about twelve, by an **anonymaous Spaniard** of the Sevilian school.

N.º 2555, *The Annunciation of the Virgin*, by **Antonio Pereda** (1608-1678).

N.º 860, *The Birth of the Virgin*, a beautiful picture, showing influences of **Velázquez,** by **J. Leonardo** (1605-1650), an Aragonese specialist in historical pieces, some of whose work we have seen in the entrance rotunda on the Main Floor.

N.º 620, *Trial of a soul*, by **Mateo Cerezo,** author of the above-mentioned *St. Augustine.*

N.º 1047, *Ecce-Homo*, or Christ the Man of Sorrows, signed by **Pereda** in 1641.

N.º 1129, *The Adoration of the Magi*, and **N.º 1130,** *The Presentation in the Temple*, both by **Francisco Rizi de Guevara.**

N.º 2583, *The Child Jesus, at the door of the Temple* (Plate 85), by **Claudio Coello** (1642-1693).

ROOM LXV.—SPANISH PAINTERS OF
THE 17TH CENTURY

Here there are a number of works of the first period of the Spanish realist school, which were formerly in the Central Gallery.

First of all.

N.º 666, *Vision of Ezechiel, the resurrection of the flesh*, by the Madrid painter **Francisco Collantes** (1599-1656).

N.º 2595, *A gentleman*, half-length, portrait with ruff and gloves, a work full of naturalness, comes from the Casa de Altamira.

N.ᵒˢ 702 and **703,** two still-lifes: *Apples, grapes and pears* and *Fruit piece*, attributed to **Juan de Espinosa** (d. 1653).

N.º 1046, *St. Jerome* (Plate 40), by **Pereda,** sigued by the artist.

Next come two naval battle-pieces: **N.º 1154,** *Seafight between Spaniards and Turks*, and **N.º 1156,** *Landing and combat*, by Captain **Juan de Toledo** (1611-1665).

N.º 1164, *Still-life*, which, like **N.º 2877,** *Offering to Pomona*, in another part of this room, is by **Juan van der Hamen,** born in Madrid in 1596, died 1631.

N.º 1020, *Return to the sheepfold*, by the Albacete painter **Pedro de Orrente** (d. 1645).

N.º 701, *St. John the Baptist*, by **Jerónimo J. Espinosa** (1600-1667), a Valencian.

N.º 67, *St. Sebastian*, attributed to **Vizencio Carducci** or **Carducho** (1576-1638), a Florentine who came to Spain when almost a child and died in Madrid. We have seen several historical paintings of his in the entrance vestibule of the Main Floor.

Finally, **N.º 665,** *Doña Mariana de Austria*, Queen of Spain, widow of Philip IV, attributed to **Claudio Coello** (1624-1693).

ROOM LXVI.—DAVID TENIERS II «THE YOUNGER»

This painter was baptized at Antwerp in 1610 and died at Brussels in 1690. Following the manner of his father, he painted small pictures full of the popular, bucolic gaiety of the common people. He departs from this line in three religious works, **N.ᵒˢ 1820, 1821** and **1822,** entitled *The temptations of St. Anthony Abbot.*

Next come **N.ᵒˢ 1802** and **1803,** *Surgical operation;* **N.º 1804,** *The alchemist;* **N.º 1813,** *Archduke Leopold William in his Brussels picture gallery;* the Archduke is shown covered, and four gentlemen uncovered; Madrazo says that these includete the Count of Fuensalida and Teniers himself, the latter being the young man.

N.º 1786, *Country festival;* **N.º 1811,** *Bivouac;* **N.º 1785,** *Village fiesta;* **N.º 1787,** *Village dance;* **N.º 1797,** *«Le roi boit»* (Plate 86).

Next come a series of small pictures, bought by Charles IV, with scenes depicting monkeys: **N.ᵒˢ 1805,** *The monkey painter;* **N.º 1806,** *The monkey sculptor;* **N.º 1807,** *Monkeys in a wine-cellar;* **N.º 1808,** *Monkeys at school;* **1809,** *Monkeys smoking,* and **N.º 1810,** *Monkey banquet.*

N.º 1799, *The nasty old man caressing the maid;* **N.º 1794, 1795** and **1796,** *Smokers and drinkers;* **N.º 1790,** *Crossbow-shooting,* and **N.º 1791,** *The jolly soldier.*

San Jerónimo.—Saint Jerome.—St.-Jerôme.—Der Heilige Hieronimus.
S. Gerolamo

**La Virgen y el Niño.—The Virgin and the Child.—La Vierge et l'Enfant.
Die heilige Jungfrau mit dem Scheafenden Christuskind.—La Madonna
con il Bambino Gesù**

Cristo en la Cruz.—Jesus Christ on the Cross.—Christ Crucifié.—Christus am Kreuze.—Cristo sulla Croce

Cacería del Tabladillo.—Hunting in the Tabladillo.—Chasse du Tabladillo.
Jagd am Tabladillo.—Caccia al Tabladillo

Jesús Niño en la puerta del Templo.—The Child Jesus at the Door of the Temple.—L'Enfant Jésus à la porte du Temple.—Christuskind am Tempel Tor.—Gesù Bambino alla porta del Tempio

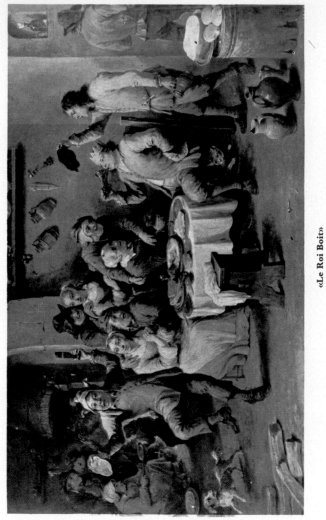

«Le Roi Boit»

El Tránsito de la Virgen.—The Death of Our Lady.—La Dormition de la Vierge.—Der Tod der Heiligen Jungfrau.—L'Assunzione della Madonna

La Virgen y el Niño.—Virgin and Child.—La Vierge et l'Enfant.—Die Jungfrau und das Kind.—La Madonna con il Bambino Gesù

La Dama de Elche

Felipe III

Santo Domingo de Guzmán.—Saint Dominic of Guzmán.—St.-Dominique de Guzmán.—Der heilige Dominikus von Guzmán.—S. Domenico di Guzmán

Autorretrato. — Selportrait. — Autoportrait. — Sebstbildnis. — Autoritratto

**Duquesa de Toscana.—Duchess of Tuscany.—Duchesse de Toscane.
Die Herzöge von Toskanien.—La Duchessa di Toscana**

Desnudo, en la playa de Portice.—Nude, on the beacn of Portici.—Nu, a la plage de Portici.—Akbild am Strande von Portici.—Nudo, sulla spiaggia di Portici

**La Condesa de Vilches.—Countess of Vilches.—Comtesse de Vilches.
Die Gräfin von Vilches.—La Contessa di Vilches**

X Conde de Westmorland

ROOM LXVII.—JAN BRUEGHEL DE VELOURS

This artis, who was born at Brussels in 1568 and died at Antwerp in 1625, is responsible for the works we shall see in this room.

N.os **1421** and **1424,** *Flower piece;* **N.**o **1438,** *Wedding banquet;* this and **N.**os **1439** and **1441** in this room, represent country scenes of popular merrymaking.

Distributed throughout the room hang five pictures on the corporeal senses: **N.**os **1394,** *Sight;* **1395,** *Hearing;* **1396,** *Smell;* **1397,** *Taste,* and **1398,** *Touch.*

The same theme is repeated in **N.**o **1403,** *Sight and Smell,* and **N.**o **1404,** *Taste, Hearing and Touch.*

N.o **1443,** *Market and washing-place in Flanders;* **N.**o **1430,** *Landscape with windmills;* **N.**o **1432,** *Drove of animals and gypsies in a wood.*

N.o **1416** and **1417,** garlands of flowers and fruits with the Virgin and Child.

N.o **1428,** *Country excursion of Isabel Clara Eugenia;* the Sovereign Princess, with her ladies and servants, amusing herself in farm tasks, by **Jan Brueghel «the Younger»** (1601-1678).

N.o **1442,** *Weeding banquet with the Archduke and Archduchess presiding;* **N.**o **1402,** *Abundance;* **N.**o **1431,** *Landscape,* by **Brueghel de Velours.**

ROOM LXVIII.—SPANISH PAINTING OF THE 16TH CENTURY

By **Juan Correa de Vivar,** a Castilian who painted for Toledo Cathedral between 1539 and 1552, we have the following panels hung in this passage: **N.**o **673,** *St. Benedict blessing St. Maurus;* **N.**o **672,** *The Virgin, the Child* *and St. Anne;* **N.º 689,** *The Visitation;* and **N.º 671,** *The Transitus of the Virgin* (Plate 87).

By **Vicente Juan Masip, «Juan de Juanes»** (1523?-1579), we again see some panels on the life of St. Stephen: **N.º 841,** *Martyrdom of St. Stephen;* **N.º 840,** *St. Stephen led out to martyrdom;* **N.º 839,** *St. Stephen accused of blasphemy;* **N.º 849,** *Christ carrying the cross,* and **N.º 1262,** *St. Stephen ordained deacon;* this last by a pupils of the master.

N.º 1294, *The Descending of the Virgin to reward St. Ildefonso,* by the **Maestro de las Once Mil Vírgenes.**

N.º 528, *Gentleman aged 54,* by and **anonymous Spaniard.**

Lastly, **N.º 1012,** *Baptism of Christ,* by the Logroño painter who worked for Philip II, **Juan Fernández de Navarrete «el Mudo»** (1526-1579).

ROOM LXIX.—CAFETERIA

On the walls of this buffet hang four Flemish still-lifes, and the room also contains second-century sculptures of Neptune and Apollo.

The door on the right leads down to the new installations in the semi-basement.

ROOM LXX

N.º 1161, *Jesus disputing with the doctors,* by **Valdés Leal** (1622-1690).

N.º 832 A, *Pope St. Leo I, «the Great»,* by **Francisco Herrera «the Elder»** (1576-1656).

N.º 1130 A, *The Immaculate Conception,* by **Francisco Rizi** (1608-1685).

N.º 2503, *St. Jerome, penitent,* by **Antonio del Castillo** (1616-1668).

N.º 1015, The Adoration of the Shepherds, by **Pedro de Orrente** (d. 1645), and some others of lesser importance.

ROOM LXXI.—THE LADY OF ELCHE

Presiding over this room, on a pedestal and under glass, we see the marvellous archaic bust, known the world over as the *Dama de Elche* or Lady of Elche (Plate 89). It is a beautiful head of a lady, a goddess or a priestess, wrought in limestone, yellowish as if sunburnt, with its original polychromy almost faded out. She has almond eyes, well-marked brows, a slightly pursed mouth and a broad forehead. Over the ears there are large, thick «cartwheels», and a series of necklaces with amulets hang round the neck.

The bust is a marvel of hieratic majesty and is full of expressive power. It was found in 1897 near Elche (Alicante), whence its name. Its proprietor sold it to the French archaeologist Pierre Paris, who presented it to the Louvre, and it remained there until 1941, when an exchange or works of art was arranged between the governments of the two countries, and it came to the Prado together with Marshal Soult's Immaculate Conception by **Murillo.**

From the bequest of D. Mario de Zayas, a Mexican of Spanish descent, there are a number of sculptures here, some of them rather mutilated. They include *The Venus of the bath*, squatting; *Divinized ephebos*, a Greek sculpture of the 5th century; *Sumero-Akkadian head*, *Minerva*, *Torso of Hercules*, *The Venus of the shell*, *Venus clothed*, a basalt *Hawk* with agate eyes, an Egyptian carving; *Horse's head and neck*, perhaps Athenian, of pink marble, 5th century B.C.

In the middle of the room is a marble vase with a relief of the battle between the Centaurs and the Lapithae, done with a technique similar to that of Phidias.

ROOM LXXII.—MEDALS

Four glass cases contain the collections of old medals from the Bosch Bequest. At the ends of the room are the sculptures of Charles V and his wife, and in the centre the equestrian statue of Philip III, probably by Juan de Bolonia.

The walls are hung with the following pictures:

N.º **1234 A,** *Elizabeth of France,* wife of Philip IV, dressed in white and gold, and N.º **1234,** *Philip IV and the dwarf «Soplillo»;* the King rests his right hand on the dwarf's head; both by **Rodrigo de Villandrando.**

N.º **2563,** *Doña Margarita de Austria,* wife of Philip III, by **Juan de Pantoja** (1553-1608).

N.º **1031,** *Isabel de Valois,* third wife of Philip II, copy of **Sánchez Coello** by **Pantoja.**

N.º **1138,** *Princesses Isabel Clara Eugenia and Catalina Micaela, daughters of Philip II,* by **Sánchez Coello.**

N.º **861,** *Isabel Clara Eugenia and Magdalena Ruiz,* by a pupil of **Sánchez Coello.**

N.º **2562,** *Philip III* (Plate 90), companion to N.º **2563,** by the same painter.

Dispersed throughout the room are several flower-pieces by **Bartolomé Pérez** (1634-1693), a Madrid painter, and **Juan de Arellano** (1614-1673).

ROOM LXXIII.—TREASURE OF THE DAUPHIN

This Room shows the important collection known as the «Treasure of the Dauphin». It consists of a valuable set of jewels and ceramics, totalling 120 pieces, finely wrought by French and Italian craftsmen during the 16th and 17th centuries, of which the most outstanding items are the pieces of tableware, decorations, rock crystal pieces and trays.

The whole belonged to Philip V and was inherited by him on the death of his father the Dauphin in 1712, son of Louis XIV. This valuable collection was kept for a long time in the Royal Palace of La Granja. The pieces are mounted and set with precious metals and stones including diamonds, emeralds, turquoises, rubies, jasper, agate and jade.

Charles III had them suitably installed in the Prado. During the War of Independence (Peninsular War) some pieces were stolen and others damaged. The treasure was restored to its place in 1815, and after restoration work was installed permanently in this Room.

Finally, in the middle of the room there is a valuable Sèvres porcelain jar, presented by Napoleon III to Isabella II in 1865.

ROOM LXXIV.—ROTUNDA DE ARIADNA

This room takes name from the large statue of Ariadne in front of the window which throws light on it. The room contains six canvases.

N.º 2593, *St. Jerome*, in cardinal's robes; a lion at his feet, and in the upper portion two angels bearing the cardinal's hat. This, and **N.º 2582,** *A martyr of the*

Hieronymite Order, are by the Sevilian painter **Juan de Valdés Leal,** a contemporary and friend of **Murillo.**

Facing these, two others which form a pair, no doubt painted for an altar: **N.º 663,** *St. Rose of Lima*, and **N.º 662,** *St. Dominic Guzmán* (Plate 91), both by **Claudio Coello** (1642-1693), court painter to Charles II.

Next, **N.º 2561,** *Don Luis de la Cerda, 9th duke of Medinaceli*, by an **anonymous Italian.**

Lastly, **N.º 2443,** *The Immaculate Conception*, by **José Antolínez** (1635-1675), a beautiful picture of the Virgin, very suggestive in colouring, surrounded by angels.

ROOM LXXV.—RUBENS AND HIS PUPILS

In the anteroom are **N.º 1625,** *Elizabeth of France, wife of Philip IV*, daughter of Henry IV of France and Maria de' Medici, and **N.º 1624,** *Maria de' Medici, queen of France*, mother of the foregoing, both by **Frans Pourbus** (d. 1622), Flemish school.

N.º 2564, *Portrait of child*, and Italian work attributed to **Giovanni Bernardo Carboni** (1614-1683); **N.º 1529,** *Still-life with a dog and cat*, by **Jan Fyt** (1611-1661); **N.º 1472,** *Don Fernando de Austria*, son of Philip III, by **Gaspar de Crayer** (1584-1669), Flemish school; and lastly, **N.º 1758,** *Concert of birds*, by Snyders.

On entering the large room, we see several mythological pictures by **Rubens,** his pupils and imitators; these are decorative canvases done for the saloons of the Real Sitio de El Pardo.

N.º 1714, *Apollo pursuing Daphne*, by **Jan Eyck,** Flemish painter; **N.º 1711,** *Hercules killing the dragon in the Garden of the Hesperides*, copied from **Rubens** by **Martínez del Mazo; N.º 1632,** *Cupid astride a dolphin*, by **Quellyn** (1607-1678); **N.º 1667,** *Orpheus and Eurydice*, by **Rubens;**

N.º **1715,** *Andromeda,* anonymous copy of **Rubens; N.º 1668,** *The Birth of the Milky Way,* by **Rubens;** N.º **1551,** *Apollo victorius over Marsyas,* by **Jordaens, N.º 1664,** *Ceres and two nymphs,* by **Rubens; N.º 1862,** *The birth of Venus,* by **Cornelius de Vos; N.º 1345,** *The fall of Phaëthon,* by **Jan Eyck; N.º 1631,** *Jason, leader of the Argonauts,* and N.º **1630,** *The death of Eurydice,* both by **Quellyn,** and N.º **1540,** *The Fall of Icarus,* by **J. P. Gowi.**

N.º **1543,** *The judgement of Solomon;* **N.º 1675,** *The goddess Flora;* **N.º 1658,** *The rape of Hippodamia* or *Lapithae and Centaurs,* and **N.º 1660,** *The banquet of Tereus.* All by **Rubens.**

N.º **1464,** *Prometheus descending to Earth,* by the Flemish painter **Jan Cossier** (1600-1671); **N.º 1659,** *The rape of Persephone,* by **Rubens.**

N.º **1369,** *Apotheosis of Hercules,* by the Flemish painter **Jan Baptiste Borkens** (1611-1675).

N.º **1633,** *Two angels driwing away evil spirits,* by **Quellyn.**

Finally, **N.º 1971,** *Cephalus and Procris,* by **Peeter Symons,** Flemish school.

ROOMS LXXVI and LXXVII.—(Offices)

ROOM LXXVIII.—(Under alteration)

ROOM LXXIX.—SOUTH STAIRCASE

While going up this staircase to the main floor, one can see the following pictures:

N.º **1844,** *Orpheus,* by **Van Tulden** and **Franz Snyders.**

N.º **473,** *The death of Cleopatra,* by **A. Vaccaro** (1598-1670); **N.º 226,** *Judith,* copy by **Guido Reni** of the original in the Spada Gallery, Rome; **N.º 53 A,** *The thanks-*

giving of Tobias, by the Italian painter **Giovanni Biliverti** (1576-1644).

N.º 2326, *Philip Von horseback*, by **Jean Ranc** (1674-1735); **N.º 1503,** *Christina of Sweden on horseback*, by **Sebastián Bourdon** (1616-1671), French school.

N.º 466, *The penitent Magdalene*, by the Napolitan **Andrea Vaccaro** (1598-1670).

Outstanding in this staircase is **N.º 1940,** *Beheading of St. John the Baptist*, by an **anonymous Fleming.** Apart from its remarkable size (12 × 30 feet), it has the peculiarity that the scene is composed with glaring anachronisms of clothing; there are figures whose faces are caricatures of historical persons of the 17th century such as Wallenstein, Henry IV of France and Ferdinand II; and it has been stated that the head of the Baptist resembles Charles I of England.

UPPER FLOOR

(South Wing)

ROOM LXXX.—MENGS

Antonio Rafael Mengs (1728-1779) occupies an important place in 18 th-century art. Painter and writer, friend of **Maella** and patron of **Goya,** he was highly esteemed by Philip V, who commissioned him to decorate the rooms of the Palace in Madrid with a series of frescoes. **Mengs** is a very careful, cultivated painter, with classical and intelectual preoccupations for the improvement of his art, a thing which he generally fails to achieve. He wrote learned articles and treatises that earned him a prestige he did not deserve, and some called him the philosopher-painter. His work is very academic and over-detailed, and themes are almost always frigid and lifeless, much the same as those of **Van Loo** or **Ranc.** The Prado contains a large collection of his pictures, which we will now enumerate.

On religious subjects there are the following: **N.º 2205,** *The penitent Magdalene;* **N.º 2206,** *St. Peter preaching;* and **N.º 2204,** *Adoration of the Shepherds.* The last-named is perhaps better than the others, and has the peculiarity that the figure just behind St. Joseph is a self-portrait. There are also two sketches of apostles, which plainly show the artist's frigidity in religious themes.

N.º 2197, *Self-portrait* (Plate 92), followed by a series of portraits of contemporary royalties: **N.º 2186,** *María Josefa of Lorraine;* **N.º 2188,** *Charles IV when a prince*, in hunting dress; **N.º 2189,** *María Luisa de Parma, Princess of Asturias;* **N.º 2200,** *King Charles III;* **N.º 2194,** *María*

Carolina of Lorraine, Queen of Naples; **N.**ᵒˢ **2198** and **2199**
(Plate 93), *The Duke and Duchess of Tuscany;* **N.**º **2201,**
Queen María Antonia of Saxony, who married the future
Charles III of Spain; **N.**º **2193,** *The Archduchess Teresa
of Austria,* depicted with a parrot; **N.**º **2191,** *Archduke
Francis of Austria;* **N.**º **2187,** *The Infante Don Antonio Pas-
cual;* **N.**º **2195,** *The Infante Don Javier de Borbón;* **N.**º **2196,**
The Infante Don Gabriel de Borbón: these last are the three
sons of Charles III.

    N.º **2191,** *Archduke Francis of Austria,* grandson of
Charles III; he later became Emperor as Francis II,
and was father-in-law to Napoleon.

    N.º **2190,** *Ferdinand IV, King of Naples,* son of Char-
les III, whom he succeeded on that throne by cession
from his father.

    N.º **2568,** *María Luisa de Parma.* Unfinished canvas,
a sketch from the life for the portrait now in the Metro-
politan Museum, New York.

    N.º **2473,** portrait of *Anna von Muralt,* by the paint-
ress of the German school **Angelica Kauffmann** (1741-
1807).

    N.º **48,** *A traveller in Italy,* by **Pompeo Battoni** (1708-
1787).

ROOM LXXXI.—DRAWINGS

    This number really applies to a passage containing
drawings and pastels by several artists; some belong to
the bequest of don Pedro Fernández Durán, who donated
them to the Prado in 1930.

    Among the drawings, we would single out for firm-
ness and perfection those of **Alonso Cano,** the 17th-
century Granada painter and sculptor, who has been
already mentioned in our tour of the lower floor.

The drawing on vellum of the Toledo church of San Juan de los Reyes by **J. Guas** is an exceptionally fine work of the end of the 15th century. We also see those by **Antonio del Castillo,** with some of his other works, as well as some pictures by **Lorenzo Tiepolo** beside those of his father **Giovanni Battista**, the decorator and fresco painter of the royal palaces, some of whose works we have already viewed; some more drawings by painters of the Madrid school; and one by **Murillo.**

Again, there are further works by **Rafael Mengs,** a painter of ingeniousness rather than genius, as Madrazo observed; two good studies by **Antonio del Castillo** and **Francisco Bayeu;** pastels by a pupil of **Mengs** and by **Vicente López;** and other works of lesser importance.

Next comes an unnumbered room which leads to the elevator and contains works by the **Bassanos** and **Lucca Giordano,** two pictures from the studio of **Titian,** and some others by 17th-century artists.

ROOM LXXXII.—19TH-CENTURY SPANISH PAINTING

This room shows some works —part of the Ramón de Errazu Bequest— by **Mariano Fortuny** (1838-1874), a Spanish painter born at Reus (Tarragona), who lived much of his life at Rome. The outstanding work in this notable collection is **N.º 2606,** a beautiful and perfect, *Nude, on the beach of Portici* (Plate 94). **N.ºs 2607** and **2608,** Moroccan types, signed by the author; **N.º 2605,** *Fantasy of Faust;* **N.º 2609,** *Idyll;* **N.º 2612,** *Old man nude in the sun*, rather more than half-length; **N.º 2627,**

Landscape, perhaps one of his last watercolours; **N.º 2610,** *Flowers;* **N.º 2931,** *The painter's children*, portrayed in the *Japanese drawing-room;* and **N.º 2611,** *Menippus*, a copy of **Velázquez's** picture on the same theme.

Another good Spanish painter is **Raimundo de Madrazo** (1841-1920), by whom we notice specially **N.º 2620,** *Gypsy woman;* **N.º 2621,** *The mannequin Alice Masson in white mantilla*, and **N.º 2622,** *Aline Masson* again; but these are surpassed by the fine head, painted from the life, **N.º 2619,** of *The Queen-Regent Doña María Cristina of Hapsburg*, clad in black with two medals; the canvas is dated 1887 at Aranjuez.

We have next, works by **Martín Rico** (1833-1908), a Madrid artist who specialized in landscapes: **N.º 2623,** *The Tower of the Ladies in the Alhambra;* **N.º 2625,** *Venice;* and a Sevilian landscape, plus some others.

Finally, we notice a fine portrait, **N.º 2628,** of the *Marquesa de Manzanedo*, seated, wearing a white dress, by the French painter **J. L. Meissonier** (1815-1891).

ROOM LXXXIII.—SPANISH PAINTING

This room contains works which are by painters that we have already met but which, for reasons of space, could not be hung beside their principal pictures. In view of the elementary character of this book, we shall merely notice them briefly.

N.º 633, *Two kings of Spain*, a companion picture to **N.º 632** in Room LXIII, by **Alonso Cano,** though some, not without reason, believe it to be by **J. Leonardo.**

Two landscapes by **Benito Manuel Agüero** (1626?-1670?), a pupil of **Martínez del Mazo,** Madrid school: **N.º 890,** *A fortified harbour;* **N.º 891,** *The Monastery of El Escorial;* **N.º 892,** *El Campillo, country house of the monks* *of El Escorial;* and one or two more, all of which have got darkened in tone.

Pentecost, by **Juan Bautista Maino,** which was part of the high-altar reredos in the church of San Pedro Mártir, Toledo, where the painter was a Dominican friar, with the canvas *The Adoration of the Magis* which we have sean in Room XXV of the Central Gallery.

These are followed by less interesting works of doubtful authorship, and finally by **N.º 1134,** *The Water from the Rock*, the biblical scene in which Moses with his rod makes water gush forth to slake the Israelites' thrist. This canvas was originally attributed to **Roelas** or **Giovachino Assereto,** but more recently Mayer has assigned it to **Llano de Valdés** (1675).

ROOM LXXXIV.—SPANISH PAINTERS OF THE 18TH AND 19TH CENTURIES

The first thing that draws our attention here is a number of pretty scenes from real life which recall **Watteau,** by the Madrilenian **Luis Paret Alcázar** (1746-1799), whom we have already met in Room XXXIX. **N.º 1044,** *The royal couples*, depicts a horse show at Aranjuez in the spring of 1773, which was attended by several princes and princesses, in the reign of Charles III. **N.º 1045,** *Ferdinand VII taking the oath as Prince of Asturias* at San Jerónimo el Real, Madrid, in 1789, in which the delicate execution of the characters and groups is noteworthy; and **N.ºˢ 1042** and **1043,** a pair of flower pieces from the Palace of Aranjuez.

By the brothers **Ramón** and **Francisco Bayeu** (1746-1793 and 1734-1795) we have several cartoons for tapestries, of which we notice specially **N.º 2451,** *The sausage-seller;* **N.º 2452,** *Fans and ring-cakes;* **N.º 2453,**

Country entertainment; **N.º 2522,** *The blind musician, The boy with the basket,* and *The picnic.*

Lastly, a series of minutely finished still-lifes from the Palace of Aranjuez, by **Luis Eugenio Meléndez** or **Menéndez** (1716-1780), a Spanish painter born at Naples who specialized in this genre, and other pictures of lesser importance.

Spanish and Italian drawings are temporarily on show in the glass cases.

ROOM LXXXV.—ITALIAN PAINTERS OF THE 16TH AND 17TH CENTURIES

N.º 2551, a panel painted on both sides and placed on a support. On one side, *St. Jerome in penance;* on the other, *Landscape with a huntsman,* an anonymous Italian work of about 1550.

N.º 59, *St. Jerome in meditation,* by **Antonio Campi,** and **59 a,** *The Crucifixion,* by **Vicencio Campi** (1536-1591).

N.º 476, *Charity,* with three children and an angel, from the Aranjuez Palace, by **Carlo Portelli,** a Florentine who died in 1574.

N.º 349, *St. Anne, the Virgin and the Child,* **anonymous Italian.**

N.º 348, *Christ carrying the Cross,* by **Sebastián del Piombo,** by whom we have seen another on the main floor.

N.º 294, *The Holy Family,* by **Domenico Puligo,** a Florentine (1492-1527).

N.ᵒˢ **27** and **28,** *Expulsion of the Money-changers from the Temple,* two canvases by **Jacopo da Ponte Bassano,** the father of the dynasty of painters, whose works we have seen on the main floor.

N.º **34,** *The Last Supper,* by **Francisco da Ponte Bassano,** son of the above, and **N.**ᵒˢ **40,** *The Flight into Egypt,* **33,** *Adoration of the Magi,* and **43,** *The Virgin Mary in Heaven,* the last two by **Leandro.**

ROOM LXXXVI.—17TH-CENTURY ITALIAN PAINTERS

In this room our attention is drawn to six canvases with scenes from the life of St. John the Baptist by the Italian painter **Massimo Stanzione** (1585-1656): **N.º 256,** *The Birth of the Baptist announced to Zachary.*

N.º **257,** *Preaching of the Baptist in the wilderness;* **N.º 258,** *Beheading of the Baptist;* and **N.º 291,** *The Baptist bids farewell to his parents.* By the same painter is also **N.º 259,** *Sacrifice to Bacchus.*

Another religious picture is **N.º 149,** *The Birth of St. John the Baptist,* by the Italian paintress **Artemisa Gentileschi** (1597-1651), daughter of the painter of the same surname.

By **Salvatore Rosa** (1615-1673) there is a magnificent seascape of large size: **N.º 324,** *The Gulf of Salerno.*

The following are the Neapolitan **Andrea Vaccaro** (1598-1670): **N.º 468,** *Meeting of Rebecca and Isaac;* **N.º 469,** *Passing of St. Januarius;* and **N.º 470,** *St. Rosalia of Palermo.*

By **Palma the Younger** (1544-1628) we have **N.º 271,** *David conquers Goliath,* and **N.º 272,** *The conversion of St. Paul;* both bought by Philip IV at the auction of Charles I's property in England.

By the Italian painter **Andrea Sacchi** (1599-1661) we have **N.º 3,** *Birth of St. John the Baptist.*

Finally, by **Crespi** (1557-1633), **N.º 547,** *St. Charles Borromeo and Christ dead.*

ROOM LXXXVII.—ITALIAN PAINTERS
(Continued.)

N.º **81,** *Landscape,* by the Bologna painter **Annibale Carracci** (1560-1609); **N.º 121,** *The Nativity,* a copy of **Pietro da Cortona** (1596-1670); **N.º 212,** *The Apostle St. James,* a more than half-length figure, by **Guido Reni** (1575-1642); **N.º 401,** *Cardinal Andrea de Austria,* anonymous, by a pupil of **Tintoretto; N.º 75,** *The Assumption of the Virgin,* one of the best and most beautiful pictures of **Annibale Carracci,** from the Monastery of El Escorial.

N.º **148,** *Self-portrait,* by **Artemisa Gentileschi,** whom we have already met. Her father **Orazio** is the author of **N.º 1240,** *The Child Jesus, asleep upon the Cross.*

N.º **471,** *The Resurrection of Our Lord,* by **Pietro Novelli** (1603-1647).

N.º **130,** *Appearance of the Angels to St. Jerome,* of which there exist several further copies, by **Domenico Zampieri «il Domenichino»** (1581-1641).

Two pictures **N.º 463** and **N.º 465,** on themes from the life of St. Cajetan, by A. Vaccaro, **N.º 341,** *Our Lady in meditation,* and **342,** *Our Lady with the sleeping Child;* in the first, she is shown with eyes half closed and hands folded, and in the second with the Child Jesus in her arms; they are two beautiful pictures, very delicate and devout, by **Giovanni Battista Salvi** (1605-1685), commonly known as **Sassoferrato,** the name of his birthplace. He was the creator of this type of beautiful pictures, which were very popular.

N.º **354,** *Veronica,* displaying the towel with the Face of Christ, by **Bernardo Strozzi** (1581-1644), from the royal collections. This picture was originally attributed to **Velázquez.**

Two pictures of *St. Agatha:* the first, **N.º 467,** by **A. Vaccaro,** and the second, **N.º 17,** showing her in prison, by **A. Barbalonga** (1600-1649).

Two more on religious themes: **N.º 200,** *St. Peter freed by an angel,* and **202,** *St. Augustine meditating upon the Trinity,* both by **F. G. Barbieri «il Guercino»** (1591-1665).

N.º 292, *The Holy Family with the bunch of grapes,* by **Camilo Procaccini,** of Bologna (1550-1629), and others of less importance.

N.º 385, *Portrait of an unknown lady,* attributed to **Tintoretto** or his daughter **Tintoretta.**

N.º 247, *Soldier bearing the Baptist's head,* by **Manfredi** (1580-1620).

ROOM LXXXVIII.—ITALIAN PAINTERS
(Continued.)

This is strictly the staircase which connects the entrance rotunda at the Goya door to the North wing of the upper floor. The following works by Italian artists hang on its walls:

N.º 512, *Rebecca and Eliezer,* by **Bautista Zelotti** (1526-1578); **N.º 236,** *The auspices,* by **Lanfranco** (1581-1647); **N.º 165,** *Bathsheba in the bath,* by **Lucca Giordano; N.º 44,** *Venice. Embarcation of the Doge,* by **Leandro Bassano; N.º 6,** *The Holy Family and Cardinal Ferdinando de' Medici,* by **Allory** (1535-1607); and **N.º 139,** *Battle between Romans and barbarians,* by **Falcone** (1600-1650), a Neapolitan painter who was a pupil of the Spaniard **Ribera.**

UPPER FLOOR

Rooms in the North Wing (LXXXIX to XCVIII)

ROOM LXXXIX.—FLEMISH PAINTERS OF THE LATE 16TH AND MIDDLE 17TH CENTURIES

N.º **1446,** *Landscape with the curing of the possessed man*, based on the Gospel account; N.º **1854,** *Landscape with ironworks*, making a pair with another similar landscape, N.º **1885,** all three by **Lucas van Valckenborgh** (1540-1597), a painter who specialized in this kind of subject.

N.º **1554,** Triptych composed of forty small pictures with paintings on copper of a variety of animals, with small landscape backgrounds, by **Jan van Kessel, «the Elder»** (1626-1679). Two of the series are missing, were later added by the Fernández Durán Bequest, and can be seen in Room XCVI. After this comes the whole series of still-lifes, pictures of game, hawking scenes, etc.

ROOM XC.—FLEMISH PAINTERS (Continued.)

N.º **1627,** *The Immaculate Conception*, by **Erasmus Quellyn** (1607-1678), a canvas which, though not in the same class with those of **Murillo,** is well painted, with a colouring in which the influence of his master **Rubens** is to be observed; the picture was presented by the Marqués de Leganés to Philip IV. There is another copy in the Monastery of El Escorial.

Next we come to a group of works by painters who delighted in depicting dead animals, comestibles, still-lifes and the like: second-class work.

N.º **1635,** *The quack dentist;* **1636,** *Card-players*, popular scenes, by **Theodor Rombouts** (1597-1637); two on fruit, poultry, etc., themes by **A. van Utrecht;** the series by **Frans Snyders** (1579-1651) on animals, and the still-lifes of **Peter Boel** (1622-1674).

ROOM XCI.—Under alteration

ROOM XCII.—FERNANDEZ-DURAN BEQUEST

This and the following rooms exhibit to the public the important collection of works of art forming the Fernández-Durán Bequest, which were donated by their owner to the Prado in 1930 and have been suitably installed here, except for the **Goyas,** which are at present to be found in Rooms XXXII and LVII A on the main floor. Perhaps the most important item in this collection is **N.º 2722,** *Our Lady with the Child*, by **Van der Weyden** (1399?-1464), of which several copies with slight variations are known. The next, **N.º 2725,** *Our Lady of Carondelet*, a copy from **van Orley** attributed to **Rubens.**

N.º **2724,** *The wise and foolish virgins*, based on the Gospel parable, is by an **anonymous Fleming,** akin to the art of **Otto van Venius,** the master of **Rubens.**

N.º **2770,** *Ecce Homo*, by the Extremaduran painter **Luis Morales** (1500-1586), some of whose works we have already seen, and lastly five small panels depicting *The Scourging, The Descending from the Cross, The Annunciation, St. Jerome*, and *Rest on the Flight into Egypt*, by **Marcellus Coffermans** (1549-1575).

ROOM XCIII.—FERNANDEZ-DURAN BEQUEST
(Continued.)

This is small corridor, in which we can see Italian drawings of the 16th and 17th centuries and collections of Chinese, English and French porcelain in the glass cases.

ROOM XCIV.—FERNANDEZ-DURAN BEQUEST
(Continued.)

Contains portraits, N.º **2793,** of *Lady María Josefa Drummond, Countess of Castelblanco,* and N.º **2794,** of her husband *Don José de Rozas,* by **Jean Baptiste Oudry,** a painter of the French school (1686-1755).

There are also one drawing by **Tiepolo,** two themes by **Carnicero,** portraits of the French school, a water-colour by **Eugenio Lucas,** porcelain from Alcora, the Royal Factory, Saxony, La Granja, Marseilles, etc., some tapestry cartoons by **Corrado Giaquinto** (1700-1765) and others.

ROOM XCV.—FERNANDEZ-DURAN BEQUEST
(Continued.)

Here we have twin *Battlepieces,* N.ºˢ **2775** and **2776,** by Captain **Juan de Toledo** (1611-1665).

N.º **2728,** *Our Lady with the Child within a festoon of fruits,* by the Fleming **Joris van Son** (1623-1667).

N.º **2733,** *Landscape with Flora, Mercury and nymphs,* by **Wildens** (1586-1637).

N.º **2788,** *The denial of St. Peter*, a large-sized picture in which the influence of **Caravaggio** is descernible.

There are also some still-lifes and landscapes of minor
importance.

ROOM XCVI.—FERNANDEZ-DURAN BEQUEST
(Continued.)

N.º **2759,** *The medical Saints Cosmas and Damian*, a
picture with contrasts of light and shade, similar to the
one in the Berlin Museum, by **Giovanni Battista Carac-
ciolo** (1570-1637).

N.º **2753,** *Still-life*, signed by the Dutch artist **Pieter
Claeszon** (1598-1661).

N.ᵒˢ **2754, 2755** and **2756,** *Still-lifes*, all by **Willem
Klaesz Heda,** also Dutch (1594 to between 1680 and
1682).

ROOM XCVII.—WORKS BY FRENCH PAINTERS
OF THE 17TH AND 18TH
CENTURIES

These works supplement the series of French paintings in Rooms XXXIII and XXXIV on the main floor.

N.º **2247,** *Susanna accused of adultery*, by **Alaine Coypel**
(1661-1722); N.º **2346,** *Martyrdom of St. Lawrence*, by
Jean de Boulogne, «el Valentín» (1594-1632).

N.º **2256,** *Landscape with an anchorite*, and N.º **2258,**
Landscape with the temptations of St. Anthony Abbot, both
by **Claude «de Lorrain»,** some of whose works we have
already seen.

N.º **2315,** *Fight between gladiators*, by **N. Poussin**
(1594-1665), a canvas in a poor state of preservation and

of doubtful authorship, and **N.º 2316,** *Anchorite among ruins,* by a pupil of **N. Poussin.**

N.º 2359, *Bacchanal,* was the front portion of a clavichord; it was originally attributed to **Poussin,** but has now been shown to be the work of one of his pupils, possibly **Gerard Lairesse** (1640-1744).

N.º 2274, *The second Mademoiselle de Blois, as Leda,* by **Pierre Gobert** (1662-1744), depicts Françoise Marie, the legitimized daughter of Louis XIV and Madame de la Montespan, at the edge of a lake, surrounded by servants and cupids.

N.º 2267, another *Bacchanal,* by **Michel-Angel Houasse,** a French painter who worked for Philip V and came to Madrid in 1719, and **N.º 2268,** *Sacrifice to Bacchus,* by the same. Both come from La Granja.

N.ᵒˢ 2270, *Saxon peasant woman in the kitchen,* and **2271,** *A villager,* by **François Hutin** (1715-1776).

Llastly, **N.º 2237,** *St. Paul and St. Barnabas at Lystra,* based on the passage in the Acts of the Apostles, by **Sébastien Bourdon** (1616-1671); **N.º 2272,** *The Magnificat,* depicting the moment when the Virgin Mary was visited by her cousin St. Elizabeth and pronounced that canticle, by **J. B. Jouvenet** (1644-1717); and other works of less importance.

ROOM XCVIII.—SPANISH PAINTERS OF THE 19TH CENTURY

N.º 863, Portrait of *Queen María Isabel de Braganza,* second wife of Ferdinand VII, by **Bernardo López Piquer** (1800-1874), a Valencian, the son and pupil of **Vicente López Portaña** and a follower of his father's technique; the Queen is seen pointing with one hand to the Prado Building, visible through the window, while the plans of it and for the hanging of the pictures can be seen on a side table.

Portraits of *Don José Gutiérrez de los Ríos* and *Señora Delicado de Imaz*, by **Vicente López; N.º 2812,** *Doña Cecilia Santos*, painted about 1840, by **Bernardo López.**

By **José de Madrazo,** a painter whose name is closely associated with the Prado, of which he was director from August 1838 to 1857, we have **N.º 2879,** portrait of *Don Gonzalo José de Vilches y Praga, Count of Vilches.*

By **Federico Madrazo** (1815-1894), who was also a director of the Prado and is undoubtedly the best painter in the Madrazo family, we have three suggestive canvases: **N.º 2878,** *Doña Amalia de Llano y Dotrés, Countess of Vilches* (Plate 95), the Count and Countess of Eleta, and **N.º 2959,** *Señora de Creus*, by **Luis de Madrazo,** and lastly, by **Raimundo de Madrazo** (1841-1920), **N.º 2603,** *The Marquesa de Manzanedo*, in a very luxurious frame, and *Doña Manuela de Errazu.*

Antonio de Esquivel (1806-1857) is the author of the portrait of *Doña Pilar de Jandiola.* **N.º 2560,** *Lady in low-necked gown*, by **J. Manuel Fernández Cruzado,** a half-length portrait of a lady wearing a «three-powers» coiffure and carrying a fan; **N.º 2904,** *Don Manuel José Quintana*, half-length of the poet, in his youth, by **José Ribelles** (1778-1835).

Lastly, we notice some recent acquisitions: portrait of *The Marquesa de San Carlos de Pedroso*, by the painter of the French school **F. E. Giacomotti,** and that of the American paintress *Mrs. Alice Lolita Muth Ben Maacha*, by **Ignacio Zuloaga.**

LOWER FLOOR, SEMI-BASEMENT

From Room LXIX, used as buffet, in which we have seen two fine sculptures of Apollo and Neptune assigned to the second century, we go down, through the door on the right, to the new installation; here the semi-basement has been fitted up as a lectureroom, in which temporary exhibitions will also be held.

ROOM XCIX.—STAIRCASE

On these walls hangs a series of twelve pictures of the *History of Rainaldo and Armida*, based on Tasso's *Gerusalemme Libertada*, by **David Teniers** (1582-1649), some of whose works we have already seen. The present set comes from the Isabel de Farnesio collection.

These are followed by landscapes by **Adries Both** and **Johannes Both,** Dutch painters of landscapes and country scenes.

There are also the portraits **N.º 1954,** *James I of England*, by **Paul van Somer** (1576-1621), **N.º 2407,** *Charles II of England*, and **N.º 2410,** *James II of England;* the last two are by **anonymous English** artists.

ROOM C.—ENGLISH PAINTERS

N.º 2858, *Portrait of an ecclesiastic*, unidentified, half-length, and that of *Mr. James Bourdien*, by the greatest of English portrait-painters **Joshua Reynolds** (1723-1792); those of *Dr. Isaac Sequeira* and *Robert Butcher*, both by the painter of the same school **Thomas Gainsbor-**

ough; a marvellous portrait, with brilliant colouring, by **Thomas Lawrence** (1769-1830) of *The Tenth Earl of Westmoreland* (Plate 96).

Next comes **N.º 2584,** *An English gentleman*, with a straw hat under his arm, by **George Romney** (1734-1802), who is also the author of *The child Master Ward*.

These are followed by two landscapes: **N.º 2852,** *The Tower of the Gold* (Seville), and **N.º 2853,** *The Castle of Alcalá de Guadaira*, by **David Roberts** (1796-1864), an artist who specialized in Andalusian themes.

Among other canvases of lesser interest, the magnificent *Portrait of a gentleman*, by **Sir John Watson Gordon** (1790-1864), is conspicuous.

ROOM CI.—DUTCH PAINTERS

This contains works by various Flemish artists. Among several landscapes and seascapes, we notice also **N.º 2106,** *Dutch lady*, by **M. Mierevelt** (1567-1641).

N.º 1986, *Release of prisoners*, by **Willem van Herb** (1614-1677).

N.º 2293, *Episcopal blessing*, by the Fleming **F. Pourbus** (1569-1622).

ROOM CII.—DUTCH PAINTERS

In conclusion, we arrive at this room, where several specimens of Dutch painting are to be seen.

N.º 2557, *A general*, by **Adrian Backer** (1638-1684); **N.º 2120,** *Cavalry encounter*, by **Van der Neer** (1634-1703); **N.º 2167,** *Portrait of J. van Olcenburnevelt*, **anonymous Dutch; N.º 127,** *Roman charity*, by **Mateo Stomer** (17th cent.); **N.º 2088,** *Apollo before the tribunal of the gods*, by **Van Harlem** (1562-1636); and **N.º 1555,** *Banquet of soldiers and courtesans*, by **C. van der Lamen.**

INDEX OF NAMES OF PAINTERS

Showing schools to which they belong, and pages
on which they are mentioned.

INDEX OF ILLUSTRATIONS

PLATES IN COLOUR

PLATES IN BLACK-AND-WHITE

CONTENTS

MAIN FLOOR

Page

LOWER FLOOR

UPPER   FLOOR
(South Wing)

Picture Galleries
in
MADRID

by **BERNARDINO DE PANTORBA**
translated by John Macnab

The only book which includes
besides the masterpieces in the

PRADO
those in other Madrid galleries:

**Museum of the Academy of San Fernando
Chapel of San Antonio de La Florida
The Lázaro Galdiano Museum
The Romantic Museum
The Museum of Modern Art
The Sorolla Museum**

and

The Museum of Contemporary Art

A critical and historical study in one volume with 126
dages of text, 208 rotogravure, 83 photogravure and 33
colour plates.